Foundations of Instructional and Performance Technology

Seung Youn Chyung

HRD Press, Inc. • Amherst • Massachusetts

Published by: HRD Press, Inc.
               22 Amherst Road
               Amherst, MA 01002
               1-800-822-2801 (U.S. and Canada)
               413-253-3488
               413-253-3490 (fax)
               www.hrdpress.com

ISBN 978-1-59996-136-1

Cover design by Eileen Klockars
Editorial services by Suzanne Bay and Sally Farnham
Production services by Anctil Virtual Office

Table of Contents

Preface

The field of human performance technology emerged from its parent field of instructional technology, based on the realization that instruction is not a cost-effective solution to *all* performance problems. Because of this historical relationship between the two fields and the fact that they are built on similar operational principles (such as systematic and systemic approaches to solving problems), one good way to learn about the two related fields is to study their historical and theoretical foundations. That is how my colleagues and I in the Department of Instructional and Performance Technology (IPT) at Boise State University educate our students in the first semester of their master's degree and certificate programs.

I started teaching a Foundations of Instructional and Performance Technology course at Boise State University in the fall of 1996. As the title of the course implies, the main goal of the course is to help new students successfully build foundational knowledge about the fields of instructional technology and human performance technology. I was hoping to find a textbook that would help students gain a good understanding about the historical and theoretical foundations of the two related fields, but no available texts seemed to serve the purpose. The only available option left to me was to provide students with a collection of published articles and book chapters. However, students had difficulty making connections among some of the articles written by different authors because formats and tones of voice were so varied. I spent a considerable amount of time each year helping students combine and synthesize the information from different sources. After doing so for ten years, I realized that my lecture-notes files became thick enough to be converted to a book! I finally decided to write a textbook so that our students would have an overview of the development of foundational principles and practices of the fields of instructional technology and human performance technology in one coherent voice. In this book I also included statements from original sources so that students will have an opportunity to learn about the ideas of original thinkers from their own words. The intended audience for this book includes students who are studying instructional technology, human performance technology, human resource development, and related subjects, as well as practitioners in the field.

There are eleven chapters in this book, and the themes of the chapters progress from the focus of instructional technology to the focus of human performance technology. Chapter 1 provides definitions of instructional technology and several important terms. Chapter 2 provides an overview of the development of the foundational principles of human learning and teaching and of systematic instructional design processes by introducing the works of important theorists such as E. L. Thorndike, Ralph Tyler, B. F. Skinner, and Benjamin Bloom. Chapter 3 reviews several individuals' contributions to the development of instructional theories and systematic instructional design processes, including the ideas of Robert Gagné, Robert Mager, Walter Dick and Lou Carey, and John Keller. Chapter 4 introduces systematic and systemic approaches to evaluating the effectiveness of training programs, using Donald Kirkpatrick's four-level model of evaluation. Chapter 5 describes the primary structure of such instructional systems development processes as the ADDIE model, and explains the meaning of the term *training needs assessment* from a historical perspective as it relates to the paradigm shift from training focus to performance focus.

Beginning with Chapter 6, the focus shifts to human performance technology. Chapter 6 clarifies the difference between behavior and performance, and introduces human performance technology as a field of study. Chapter 7 provides an overview of Thomas Gilbert's leisurely theorems, covering the concepts of worthy performance, potential for improving performance, and the behavior engineering model. Chapter 8 describes the process of front-end analysis as Joe Harless defines it. Chapter 9 provides an overview of Roger Kaufman's organizational elements model, which identifies five elements of a system and the interrelationships among them. Chapter 10 provides an overview of several theories and studies derived from the fields of industrial and organizational psychology and social psychology, such as Frederick Taylor's scientific management theory, the Hawthorne studies, Kurt Lewin's field theory, and Frederick Herzberg's motivation-hygiene theory. These theories and research findings have a substantial impact on and implications for current human performance technology practice, as they relate to understanding human behavior and improving performance in work environments. Chapter 11 provides a summary of the historical and theoretical relationships between the field of instructional technology and the field of human performance technology.

This book certainly does not cover an exhaustive list of topics necessary to build complete foundations of the fields of instructional technology and human performance technology. The topics included in this book were chosen for students who are fairly new to the fields to help them build the initial layers of theoretical and historical foundations within a semester-long period of time. Instructors who adopt this book as a textbook for their courses might choose to assign chapters and related articles listed in the chapter references as weekly reading assignments. Instructors should consider assigning small real-life projects to reinforce student understanding of the foundational principles of instructional design and performance improvement gained from the reading assignments.

Chyung
2008

Acknowledgments

Many people helped me while writing this book. First, I would like to thank students of IPT 536 Foundations of Instructional and Performance Technology class at Boise State University for providing me with feedback on a draft version of this book. I especially wish to acknowledge IPT students and graduates Paula Anderson, Shelley Berg, Christina Caswell, Jay Lambert, Joanne Letourneau, Maurreen Stebner, and Kelly Weak for allowing me to use their class projects as examples. I also thank Ms. Marilyn Gilbert for reviewing the manuscript and providing me with helpful feedback on the chapter covering Thomas Gilbert's work. Special thanks go to Shelley Berg, my graduate assistant, who helped me revise the manuscript, and Dr. Donald Winiecki for giving me constant support, encouragement, and suggestions, and for designing the images included in this book.

Chapter

1

Technology and Instructional Technology

Technology and Instructional Technology

Definition of technology	**tech·nol·o·gy** \ˌtek-ˈnä-lə-jē\ *n, pl* **-gies** [Gk *technologia* systematic treatment of an art, fr. *tekhnē* art, skill + *-o-* + *-logia* -logy]

     1: a: the practical application of knowledge esp. in a particular area:
            ENGINEERING <medical ~>
         b: a capability given by the practical application of knowledge
            <a car's fuel saving ~>
     2: a manner of accomplishing a task esp. using technical processes,
        methods, or knowledge <new *technologies* for information storage>
     3: the specialized aspects of a particular field of endeavor
        <educational ~> **-tech·nol·o·gist** \-jist\ *n*

(Merriam-Webster's Collegiate Dictionary, 2003, p. 1283)

What is instructional technology?	Ask people on the streets what instructional technology means to them. Their responses will vary, but their definitions are likely to be associated with either media devices or design processes that make things better.

One of the early definitions of instructional technology was published by the Commission on Instructional Technology in 1970:

> Instructional technology can be defined in two ways. In its more familiar sense, it means the media born of the communications revolution which can be used for instructional purposes alongside the teacher, textbook, and blackboard. . . . The second and less familiar definition of instructional technology goes beyond any particular medium or device. In this sense, instructional technology is more than the sum of its parts. It is a systematic way of designing, carrying out, and evaluating the total process of learning and teaching in terms of specific objectives, based on research in human learning and communication, and employing a combination of human and nonhuman resources to bring about more effective instruction. (p. 21)

A simple way to understand instructional technology is to think of it as a means to an end.

First, instructional technology is *end driven*. Technology is goal oriented; it aims at achieving a pre-set objective, such as solving problems or improving outcomes. Instructional technology is also goal oriented. Its main objective is to solve problems associated with human learning and instructional processes in order to produce better learning outcomes.

Second, instructional technology looks for *effective methods* to accomplish the goal. The methods can be derived from physical science concepts or behavioral science concepts. Although technology is often associated with the physical science concepts, the core concepts of instructional technology come from behavioral science concepts, as Saettler (1971) points out below:

> The most important aspect of this concept of instructional technology concerns the application of scientific knowledge to provide a conceptual basis and methodology for the design, development, and evaluation of instruction and instructional products for the purpose of improving the related components of the educational process. (p. 308)

Along with the step-by-step, *systematic* methodology for the design, development, and evaluation of instruction, a *systemic* approach should also be employed in order to understand the interacting relationships among different elements in the instructional system.

By putting it all together, Gentry (1995) offers a definition of instructional technology:

> the systemic and systematic application of strategies and techniques derived from behavior[al] and physical science concepts and other knowledge to the solution of instructional problems (p. 7)

Instructional technologists are professionals who possess expert knowledge in systemically and systematically selecting and utilizing strategies and techniques derived from behavioral and physical science concepts when attempting to solve problems associated with human learning and teaching.

Development of instructional technology

This chapter provides a brief overview of instructional technology as a field by addressing the following topics:

- When instructional technology as a field was developed
- When instructional technologists as professionals became recognized
- Where and how instructional technology started to be used
- Why instructional technology is needed
- What knowledge instructional technologists apply
- How instructional technologists use such knowledge

Readers are encouraged to keep these topics in mind throughout this book.

Who, When, *and* Where: *Instructional Technologists*

Historical overview

The foundations of instructional technology were established as responses to various influences, including world wars, the development of new instructional media, and the influence of educational psychology during the first half of the 20th century. The profession of instructional technology emerged during World War II. The roles of instructional technologists have changed over time. Instructional technology has been used in education and in training. The historical events summarized in this section are based on Cuban (1986), Reiser (1987), Saettler (1968, 1990), Shrock (1995), and other sources.

The early 20th century and World War I

During the early 20th century, educational psychologists such as E. L. Thorndike started developing theories of human learning and a technology of instruction based on empirical studies (Saettler, 1968). Also, the need for military equipment and supplies during World War I forced manufacturers to look for effective and efficient ways to train large numbers of workers. The Emergency Fleet Corporation of the United States Shipping Board, for example, had to train nearly 500,000 workers quickly. As a strategy, Charles R. Allen, the head of the program, used a structured four-step instructional technique: Show-Tell-Do-Check (Miller, 1996). It was one of the early *systematic* instructional methods used in job training.

1920s–1930s

Since the 1920s, various communication media have been adopted as "instructional media." Adoption of new communication media for classroom teaching was considered an innovative and progressive approach to instruction. Film projectors and radio were the early media used in classrooms in the United States (Cuban, 1986). Educational motion pictures were introduced into classrooms during the first decade of the 20th century. During the 1920s and 1930s, films used in classrooms were viewed as "a symbol of progressive teaching approaches" (p. 12). However, teachers did not use films as an instructional tool as frequently as was expected, because teachers lacked the skills to use the equipment, the costs were high, and the supply of appropriate films for classroom use was insufficient or nonexistent. Radio was also introduced as an instructional media in the 1920s, and was initially expected to become the "textbook of the air" (p. 19). However, radio was not fully adopted by teachers and transformed into a common instructional technology either. Reasons included unavailability of equipment, difficulties in scheduling, poor quality of equipment and reception, lack of information, and lack of curriculum-related programs. There were various organized activities and audio-visual development projects, but instructional technology was not an established field at that time.

1940s and
World War II

World War II created another emergency need to train a large number of people in industry, as well as in the military. Instructional technology emerged as a recognized profession in the United States during World War II, when the development and delivery of reliable audio-visual media and training was deemed critical to the war effort (Miller, 1996; Shrock, 1995). During that time, Vannevar Bush wrote about the implications of technology for augmenting human capabilities in a visionary article published in the July 1945 issue of *The Atlantic Monthly*. His vision influenced the work of many future scientists, including Douglas Engelbart, the inventor of the computer mouse and developer of a collaborative online system in the 1960s, and Tim Berners-Lee, the inventor of the World Wide Web in the late 1980s.

1950s–1970s

When World War II ended, television became the newest instructional media to be used in the classroom. Instructional technologists started putting more emphasis on the instructional *process* than on the *media* (Reiser, 2002). Numerous models of instructional design and theories of learning and instruction were developed. Behavioral psychology, led by E. L. Thorndike in the early 20th century and B. F. Skinner in the mid–20th century, influenced the development of a *technology of instruction*. Programmed instruction is one example (Saettler, 1968, 1990; Skinner, 1968). Instructional technologists were viewed as not only media specialists, but also instructional design experts. In the 1970s, a cognitive approach to the technology of instruction began to replace the behaviorist view (Saettler, 1990).

1980s–present

Microcomputers were introduced into classrooms in the 1980s. The unique attributes of microcomputers made it possible for learners to engage in individualized multimedia-based learning and to receive immediate feedback more easily than before. Tim Berners-Lee, a scientist at CERN (**C**onseil **E**uropéen pour la **R**echerche **N**ucléaire) in Switzerland, developed the World Wide Web in 1989, which has revolutionized the pedagogical paradigm. The Web is an instructional media, but it also has the potential to be a holistic *learning* and *performance* environment that promotes individualized and self-directed learning and facilitates collaborative learning and performance improvement.

With all of the developments of the past century, instructional technologists have greater responsibilities than ever before. Instructional technologists' responsibilities include analyzing the need for providing instruction; designing, developing, and delivering instruction; and evaluating instructional outcomes. Instructional technologists are often recognized as "learning specialists" who are concerned with *instructional* interventions and various *learning* and *performance improvement* interventions, such as job aids and Web-based performance support systems.

Why: *Linking Means to Ends*

Reactive and proactive

Why is technology used in instruction? Technology is used for several reasons:

1. To solve existing problems (reactive)
2. To prevent possible problems from happening (proactive)
3. To improve existing conditions (reactive and proactive)

Similarly, instructional technology is used for the following purposes:

1. To solve instruction-related problems that cause less-desirable learning outcomes (reactive)
2. To prevent such problems from happening so that desirable learning outcomes can be achieved (proactive)
3. To improve the quality of current learning environments (reactive and proactive)

Means and ends

Technology and instructional technology each imply the use of means to achieve end results.

- Technology is the application of scientific knowledge (i.e., the means) in order to achieve desirable goals (i.e., the ends).

- Instructional technology is the application of scientific knowledge regarding human learning and teaching (i.e., the means) in order to produce desirable learning outcomes (i.e., the ends).

Such scientific knowledge mostly comes from behavioral sciences (Saettler, 1971). Behavioral sciences such as psychology and sociology provide the field of instructional technology with credible information about human learning and performance, gained from empirical research and development.

- Learning theories and instructional theories are the core behavioral science concepts that instructional technologists frequently use during various phases of instructional development.

- Instructional technologists should also be able to understand different attributes of various delivery media in order to select and use those most appropriate for accomplishing desired ends.

What: *Using Hard and Soft Technology*

Hard and soft sides of technology

What kind of technology do instructional technologists use? Heinich, Molenda, Russell, and Smaldino (1999) explain the difference between hard technology and soft technology used in instruction:

- Hard technology is "the hardware, such as television, computers, and satellites, used as tools to provide instruction" (p. 405).

- Soft technology is "techniques and methods that form psychological and social frameworks for learning, as opposed to the hardware used to deliver instruction" (p. 409).

In other words,

- Instructional *hard* technology refers to tangible media such as audiotapes, videos, TVs, and computers used to deliver instructional messages and to communicate with learners.

- Instructional *soft* technology refers to such intangible things as instructional design processes and instructional strategies developed based on the principles of behavioral science.

Instructional media can be used *without following any specific instructional design principles*, and instructional strategies can be carried out *without using specific media technology*. However, in order to develop economical, reliable, and effective instruction and delivery systems, instructional technologists should possess knowledge of *both* hard technology and soft technology, as shown in Figure 1.

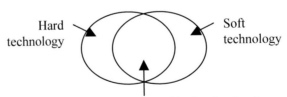

Soft technology implemented by hard technology

Figure 1. The relationship between soft technology and hard technology.

Analogy

Instructional *hard* technology can be compared to a grocery delivery vehicle that brings nutritional content to the destination (Clark, 1983, 1994). Instructional *soft* technology is the method used to package the content or to select the right type of a vehicle to deliver the content in good quality.

How: *Using Systematic and Systemic Approaches*

Systematic vs. systemic

How do instructional technologists apply their professional knowledge? Instructional technologists apply their knowledge in systematic and systemic ways. The terms *systematic* and *systemic* have different meanings.

sys·tem·at·ic \sis-tə-ˈma-tik\ *adj* 1: relating to or consisting of a system 2: presented or formulated as a coherent body of ideas or principles <~ thought> 3: a: methodical in procedure or plan <a ~ approach> <a ~ scholar> b: marked by thoroughness and regularity <~ efforts> 4: of, relating to, or concerned with classification; *specif*: TAXONOMIC	**sys·tem·ic** \sis-ˈte-mik\ *adj* : of, or relating to, or common to a system: as a: affecting the body generally b: supplying those parts of the body that receive blood through the aorta rather than through the pulmonary artery c: of, relating to, or being a pesticide that as used is harmless to the plant or higher animal but when absorbed into its sap or bloodstream makes the entire organism toxic to pests

(Merriam-Webster's Collegiate Dictionary, 2003, pp. 1269 & 1270)

Systematic approaches

Systematic applications refer to purposely planned, methodical, step-by-step approaches that are likely to lead to desirable outcomes. For example, instructional technologists:

1. recognize an existing (or potential) problem in a learning and instructional situation that should be solved;
2. investigate to identify the cause(s) of the problem, and seek a solution or a set of solutions to the problem by looking at various sources;
3. determine the most cost-effective solution(s) by using their own professional knowledge or even educated guesses, as well as research findings and other experts' opinions;
4. implement the selected solution(s); and
5. evaluate the effectiveness of the solution(s).

Systematic approaches to solving problems are often illustrated as a linear procedure between a starting point and an ending point, as shown in Figure 2:

Figure 2. A systematic approach.

In understanding the meaning of systematic approaches, it is important to recognize that an ending point should be set up before you formulate a starting point and plan for a route to reach the ending point.

In other words, in order to apply systematic approaches in instructional or performance improvement situations, one should clearly define a desired outcome or goal before designing methods or strategies to accomplish it. Without a goal in mind, no methods will function as systematic approaches. The famous quote by the Cheshire cat in Lewis Carroll's *Alice's Adventures in Wonderland*—"If you don't know where you want to go, any road will take you there"—is often used to illustrate the importance of having an end in mind when working on instructional and performance-improvement projects.

Systemic approaches	Professionals who use *systemic* applications, on the other hand, take into account networks of interrelated factors while trying to implement solutions to achieve desirable outcomes. This is because a change or a barrier in one area might have an effect on other areas.

Here are several hypothetical situations that illustrate how a change in one area can have an impact on another area:

- A new learning management system (LMS) was implemented as part of a company-wide e-learning strategy. Since then, instructional designers have been tasked to modify existing e-learning courseware products to make them run on the new LMS. Currently, about 60 percent of their time is being spent on revising existing courseware, which has resulted in failure to meet deadlines for completing other instructional design projects.
- A new instructional strategy was implemented in a training program. The staff found that it worked well for a small number of advanced learners, but not for novice learners. The group-average score on the final assessment turned out to be lower than the score from the assessment given before the new method was implemented.
- At a manufacturing factory, new hires used to be trained via instructor-led, large-group, classroom instruction. The classroom instruction was not effective because it did not incorporate hands-on practice. The classroom instruction was eventually replaced with on-the-job training (OJT). Five top performers were selected as OJT instructors. Each OJT instructor was responsible for providing one-on-one training to several new hires. Because of the increased amount of hands-on practice and one-on-one coaching, the new hires performed much better than the previous group. However, the overall production level decreased slightly because the five top performers spent most of their time providing OJT instead.

Consideration of the systemic impact of interrelated factors likely influences modification of one or more parts of a systematic procedure, as can be seen in Figure 3.

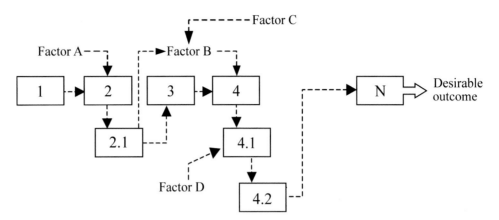

Figure 3. A systemic approach.

Analogies

Systematic approaches are like climbing up on a ladder or laying out stepping stones in a stream or developing an itinerary for a trip. It is important to first set the destination, and then to plan and follow from a starting point to an ending point.

Systemic approaches are analogous to the act of touching a spider web: touching a single strand of a spider web makes the whole web vibrate (Rothwell, 1995). Therefore, when solving a problem, it is important to look at the big picture, where you can see the interrelated factors before you begin to try to fix it.

Sometimes, instructional technologists might simply follow a systematic procedure without investigating additional systemic factors and incorporating them into their instructional design and execution. However, instructional technologists will often need to use both systematic and systemic approaches in order to produce desirable outcomes (see Figure 4).

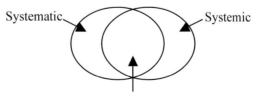

Systematic and systemic application of scientific knowledge in order to produce desirable outcomes

Figure 4. The relationship between systematic and systemic approaches.

An alternative, comprehensive look at soft technology

Systematic and systemic methods are commonly described as "soft" technology and delivery media as "hard" technology, as shown in Figure 5. There are two alternative ways to define the meaning of soft technology. First, soft technology can refer to the use of systematic and systemic methods that are effectively and efficiently delivered by media technology. That is, as shown in Figure 6, the selection and use of appropriate hard technology is seen as part of soft technology. A more comprehensive interpretation incorporates the entire processes of recognizing a situation to be addressed, applying systematic and systemic methods via media technology, and achieving a desired outcome (see Figure 7). Practitioners in the field of instructional technology are encouraged to embrace this more comprehensive interpretation of soft technology.

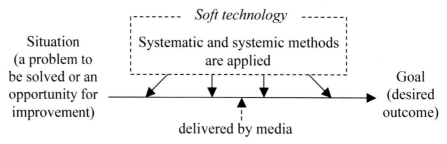

Figure 5. Soft technology = systematic and systemic methods.

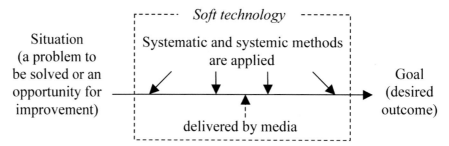

Figure 6. Soft technology = systematic and systemic methods applied and delivered by media.

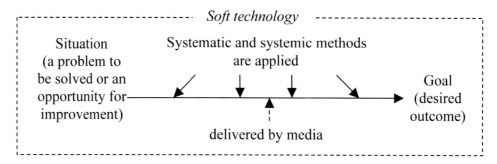

Figure 7. Soft technology = the entire process of recognizing a situation to be addressed, applying systematic and systemic methods delivered by media, and achieving a desired outcome.

References

Banathy, B. H. (1968). *Instructional systems*. Palo Alto, CA: Fearon Publishers.

Bush, V. (1945, July). As we may think. *The Atlantic Monthly, 176*(1), 101–108.

Clark, R. (1983). Reconsidering research on learning from media. *Review of Educational Research, 53*(4), 445–459.

Clark, R. (1994). Media will never influence learning. *Educational Technology Research and Development, 42*(2), 21–29.

Commission on Instructional Technology (1970). Instructional technology today (Part one: A report by the Commission on Instructional Technology). In Tickton S.G. (Ed.), *To improve learning: An evaluation of instructional technology* (Vol. I, pp. 21–27). New York: R. R. Bowker Company.

Cuban, L. (1986). *Teaching and machines: The classroom use of technology since 1920*. New York: Teachers College, Columbia University.

Gentry, C. G. (1995). Educational technology: A question of meaning. In G. Anglin (Ed.), *Instructional technology: Past, present, and future* (2nd ed., pp. 1–9). Englewood, CO: Libraries Unlimited.

Heinich, R., Molenda, M., Russell, J., & Smaldino, S. (1999). *Instructional media and technologies for learning* (6th ed.). Upper Saddle River, NJ: Prentice Hall.

Merriam-Webster's collegiate dictionary (11th ed.). (2003). Springfield, MA: Merriam-Webster.

Miller, V. A. (1996). The history of training. In R. L. Craig (Ed.), *The ASTD training & development handbook* (4th ed., pp. 3–18). New York: McGraw-Hill.

Reiser, R. (1987). Instructional technology: A history. In R. Gagné (Ed.), *Instructional technology: Foundations* (pp. 11–48). Hillsdale, NJ: Lawrence Erlbaum Associates, Inc.

Reiser, R. (2002). What field did you say you were in? Defining and naming our field. In R. A. Reiser, & J. V. Dempsey (Eds.), *Trends and issues in instructional design and technology* (pp. 5–15). Upper Saddle River, NJ: Merrill Prentice Hall.

Rothwell, W. J. (1995). Beyond training and development. *Management Review, 84*(9), 4.

Saettler, P. (1968). *A history of instructional technology*. New York: McGraw-Hill.

Saettler, P. (1971). The physical science versus the behavioral science concept of instructional technology. In Tickton S.G. (Ed.), *To improve learning: An evaluation of instructional technology* (Vol. II, pp. 307–313). New York: R. R. Bowker Company.

Saettler, P. (1990). *The evolution of American educational technology*. Englewood, CO: Libraries Unlimited, Inc.

Shrock, S. (1995). A brief history of instructional development. In G. Anglin (Ed.), *Instructional technology: Past, present, and future* (2nd ed., pp. 11–19). Englewood, CO: Libraries Unlimited.

Skinner, B. F. (1968). *The technology of teaching*. New York: Appleton-Century-Crofts.

Foundations of Instructional Development

Foundational Principles for Instructional Development

Instructional design as a prescriptive science

Instructional design is a *prescriptive science*. The main goal of instructional design is to produce effective instruction by using systematic and systemic methods. The effectiveness of instruction is measured based on whether or not the expected learning outcomes have been achieved.

Instructional design principles

Various instructional design principles can be used when developing instruction. For example, it is important to maintain **congruence** among three instructional elements:

1. Instructional objectives
2. Instructional activities
3. Assessment methods

The three elements should be carefully matched, as shown in Table 1:

Table 1. A Congruently Designed Lesson Structure

Instructional Objectives	Instructional Activities	Assessment Methods
Without using reference materials, students will be able to list the six factors of Thomas Gilbert's behavior engineering model (BEM) in the correct order.	• Show Gilbert's BEM in a table. • Explain the sequence Gilbert said should be followed. • Provide an example of the use of the six factors in the correct order to diagnose a problem.	Show the BEM table without the labels of the six factors. Ask students to write down the labels in the correct cells and then to number them in the proper order.

To achieve this congruence, instructional designers should set a cornerstone for the instructional design process, which starts with the analysis and design of instructional goals and objectives. The instructional design procedure is a soft side of instructional technology (i.e., soft technology).

Development of instructional design principles

This chapter provides an overview of the important contributions of several individuals to the development of foundational principles of human learning and teaching, and discusses systematic instructional design processes. The selected individuals are E. L. Thorndike, Ralph Tyler, B. F. Skinner, and Benjamin Bloom.

Edward Lee Thorndike (1874–1949)

Thorndike's connectionism	E. L. Thorndike, with his learning theory of connectionism and empirical research, helped create a fundamental change in the way we understand human learning and instruction. Thorndike is considered one of the early educational psychologists who provided foundational principles leading to the development of *a science and technology of instruction* (Saettler, 1968).
The scientific basis of teaching	Thorndike finished his dissertation on animal intelligence and joined the faculty of the Teachers College at Columbia University in 1899. He then started focusing on the development of a science of human learning and a technology of instruction (Saettler, 1968, 1990). Thorndike believed that the efficiency of any profession, even the profession of teaching, would largely depend on the degree to which its practitioners used scientific methods, and he advocated the use of scientific methods for testing instructional results:

> The profession of teaching will improve (1) in proportion as its members direct their daily work by the scientific spirit and methods, that is by honest, open-minded consideration of facts, by freedom from superstitions, fancies or unverified guesses, and (2) in proportion as the leaders in education direct their choices of methods by the results of scientific investigation rather than by general opinion. (Thorndike, 1906, p. 257)

Foundational principles of learning and teaching	He formulated these principles of behavioral learning and teaching:

1. **The law of effect.** An individual repeats responses that are followed by a satisfying effect, and tends not to repeat responses that are followed by an annoying state of affairs. In other words, "satisfying results strengthen, and discomfort weakens, the bond between situation and response" (Thorndike, 1912, p. 96). The satisfying and annoying effects are determined by the fulfillment or interference of the learner's "wants" (Thorndike & Gates, 1929).

2. **The law of readiness.** Readiness is a condition at a certain moment. One should be ready to act in a certain way in order to take it as a satisfying effect; otherwise, having to act in that way would be considered an annoying effect. Thus, the law of readiness and the law of effect are closely related: "The greater the readiness the more potent the operation of effect" (Thorndike & Gates, 1929, p. 93).

3. **The law of exercise.** To sustain the reaction to a satisfying effect, it needs to be repeated. Practice alone does not make perfect, but "practice which brings satisfaction, which satisfies some real wants, is what makes perfect" (Thorndike & Gates, 1929, pp. 93–94). Thorndike briefly described this law as "other things being equal, *exercise strengthens the bond between situation and response*" (Thorndike, 1912, p. 95).

A systematic process of teaching

Thorndike (1906) viewed the purpose of teaching as "to produce and to prevent changes in human beings" (p. 7) and formulated five problems that education should deal with, as presented in Table 2. He clearly addressed the importance of providing goal-oriented education and conducting evaluation.

Table 2. Thorndike's View of Education and the Implications

Five Problems (Thorndike, 1912, p. 8)	Systematic Steps Implied
1. **The aims of education.** What changes should be made in human beings?	Goal analysis
2. **The material or subjects of education.** What is the original nature of the human beings whom we have to change? What are the principles or laws of human nature and behavior that we should know in order to change men for the better?	Learner analysis and content analysis
3. **The means and agents of education.** What forces are at our command in the task of producing and preventing changes in human beings?	Environment, resource, or cause analysis
4. **The methods of education.** How should these means and agents be brought to bear upon the subjects of education so as best to realize its aims?	Design and development
5. **The results of education.** What have been the actual effects of different methods, means and agents upon different kinds of human beings?	Evaluation

Thorndike's work helped spark a paradigm shift in curriculum design. He offered principles of curriculum design that suggested that in order to achieve the desirable outcomes, specific educational goals had to be determined and instruction should be clearly linked to the achievement of the prescribed goals. Also, carefully designed individualized instruction was aimed at mastery learning, which was a different perspective than the traditional instruction that resulted in a normal curve of achievement. The instructional results were evaluated to find the cause of a problem and to facilitate continuous improvement: "To produce a desired effect, find its cause and put that in action" (Thorndike, 1912, p. 60). The causes of educational problems can be explained by behavioral science, such as Thorndike's laws of human behavior.

Thorndike also stressed the importance of effective teaching methods and activities that facilitate learners' ability to *transfer* their knowledge from one situation to another so that they can function more effectively in their own lives (Thorndike & Gates, 1929; Tyler, 1986/1987).

Ralph Winfred Tyler (1902–1994)

Influence of Thorndike's work	Many individuals followed Thorndike's footsteps and used his work as the basis for more groundbreaking ideas. Ralph Tyler was one of them. When *The 26th Yearbook of the National Society for the Study of Education* was released in the late 1920s, Tyler was so impressed by the rationale and justification for establishing a curriculum as a professional study that he decided to devote his professional career to the study and improvement of curriculum (Tyler, 1986/1987).
The Eight-Year Study (1933–1941)	During the Great Depression, a lot of young people stayed in school because job opportunities were scarce. But even after graduating from high school, they could not find jobs, and many felt that formal education did not prepare them to become self-directed adults. As a response to the problem, the Commission on the Relation of School and College of the Progressive Education Association conducted an eight-year longitudinal study with 30 private and public schools, large and small, from different sections of the nation. This study has been named *The Eight-Year Study,* and the institutional participants are known as *The Thirty Schools.* Tyler was the director of the evaluation staff for the study (Tyler, 1981, 1986/1987).

After more than a year of study, the commission concluded that secondary education in the nation was not adequate in several major aspects. Some of the issues that the commission found were:

> *Secondary education in the United States did not have [a] clear-cut, definite, central purpose. . . . Our secondary schools did not prepare adequately for the responsibilities of community life. . . . Schools failed to create conditions necessary to effective learning. . . . Principals and teachers labored earnestly, often sacrificially, but usually without any comprehensive evaluation of the results of their work. . . . Finally, the relation of school and college was unsatisfactory to both institutions.* In spite of the fact that formal education for five out of six of our youth ends at or before graduation from high school, secondary schools were still dominated by the idea of preparation for college. The curriculum was still chiefly "college preparatory." . . . Because of this, the school placed undue emphasis upon preparation for college, to the neglect of its responsibility to those who were entering directly into the life of the community. (Aikin, 1942, pp. 4–11)

As the members of the commission and the representatives of the 30 schools continued to meet to plan together, they came to articulate two major principles that they hoped would guide their efforts:

The first was that the general life of the school and methods of teaching should conform to what is now known about the ways in which human beings learn and grow. . . . Holding this view, the participating schools believed that the school should become a place in which young people work together at tasks which are clearly related to their purposes. . . . *The second major principle which guided the work of the participating schools was that the high school in the United States should re-discover its chief reason for existence.* (Aikin, 1942, pp. 17–18)

Tylerian objectives-based evaluation

The Eight-Year Study is recognized as a successful experiment in which *behavioral objectives* were effectively utilized and *continuous evaluations* were conducted to examine the effectiveness of each school's new curriculum, designed to meet the specific needs of its own students. The fact that the following seven steps were used to develop the evaluation program clearly illustrates that the evaluation was conducted based on pre-determined objectives:

1. Formulating objectives
2. Classification of objectives
3. Defining objectives in terms of behavior
4. Suggesting situations in which achievement of objectives will be shown
5. Selecting and trying promising evaluation methods
6. Developing and improving appraisal methods
7. Interpreting results (Smith, Tyler, & the evaluation staff, 1942, pp. 15–25)

Behavioral Objectives: Each school was asked to list its educational objectives. The statements of objectives obtained from the Thirty Schools were grouped into 10 major types:

1. The development of effective methods of thinking
2. The cultivation of useful work habits and study skills
3. The inculcation of social attitudes
4. The acquisition of a wide range of significant interests
5. The development of increased appreciation of music, art, literature, and other aesthetic experiences
6. The development of social sensitivity
7. The development of better personal-social adjustment
8. The acquisition of important information
9. The development of physical health
10. The development of a consistent philosophy of life (Aikin, 1942, pp. 89–90)

In doing so, Tyler laid out what was later considered to be groundbreaking work in writing behavioral objectives. Tyler (1949) explained that a clearly stated behavioral objective should be written in two dimensions: the behavioral aspect and the content aspect. He wrote:

> The most useful form for stating objectives is to express them in terms which identify both the kind of behavior to be developed in the student and the content or area of life in which this behavior is to operate (pp. 46–47). . . . They [behavioral objectives] should have been defined clearly so as to provide a concrete guide in the selection and planning of learning experiences. (p. 111)

As an example, Tyler (1949) provided seven types of behavior that progress systematically:
1. Understanding of important facts and principles
2. Familiarity with dependable sources of information
3. Ability to interpret data
4. Ability to apply principles
5. Ability to study and report results of study
6. Broad and mature interests
7. Social attitudes

Continuous Evaluations: The participating schools initially faced an inability to evaluate the outcomes of the newly developed curriculum:

> The schools were saying to the Evaluation Staff, "We do not know surely whether our work is producing the results we desire. We need to know. Can you help us find out whether or not our efforts produce in students effective methods of thinking; a wide range of significant interests; increased appreciation of music, art, and literature; social sensitivity; and a consistent philosophy of life? If our teaching is not bringing about these results, we shall change our curriculum and teaching methods in the hope that we can accomplish our purposes. Then we shall examine results again." (Aikin, 1942, p. 90)

The main task of the evaluation staff was to develop test instruments and to conduct repeated evaluations to help the participating schools identify the changes produced in students, and revise their curriculum if necessary:

> In the Thirty Schools evaluation and teaching belong together. They react upon each other continuously. Step by step in the process of learning, the teacher and student measure the distance traveled, learn just where the student is and how far he has to go to reach the desired goal. (Aikin, 1942, p. 94)

Tyler (1949) emphasized the importance of making use of the evaluation data for continuous improvement. He wrote:

> What is implied in all of this is that curriculum planning is a continuous process and that as materials and procedures are developed, they are tried out, their results appraised, their inadequacies identified, suggested improvements indicated; there is replanning, redevelopment and then reappraisal; and in this kind of continuing cycle, it is possible for the curriculum and instructional program to be continuously improved over the years. In this way we may hope to have an increasingly more effective educational program rather than depending so much upon hit and miss judgment as a basis for curriculum development. (p. 123)

About 30 years after the Eight-Year Study, Michael Scriven (1967) coined the terms *formative evaluation* and *summative evaluation*. *Formative evaluation* refers to the use of constant evaluation processes during instructional development with the intention of continuously improving the quality, whereas *summative evaluation* refers to the method of conducting a final evaluation of the project.

Basic principles of curriculum and instruction

In his book *Basic Principles of Curriculum and Instruction* (1949), Tyler summarized the rationale for viewing, analyzing, and interpreting instructional programs with four fundamental questions. He asserted that these four questions must be answered when developing any type of instructional program. As shown in Table 3, the four questions imply several major principles of instructional design which were developed subsequently by others, and are currently practiced.

Table 3. Tyler's Principles of Curriculum Design and the Implications

Four Questions (Tyler, 1949, p. 1)	Principles Implied
1. What educational purposes should the school seek to attain?	Determine instructional objectives
2. What educational experiences can be provided that are likely to attain these purposes?	Select learning experiences
3. How can these educational experiences be effectively organized?	Organize learning experiences
4. How can we determine whether these purposes are being attained?	Evaluate learning outcomes

Similar to Thorndike's idea, Tyler's emphasis on the importance of the *transfer-of-training* principle in curriculum design stressed that students should be able "to transfer what is learned in school to situations outside the school" (Tyler, 1976, p. 64).

Burrhus Frederic Skinner (1904–1990)

Behavioral
learning
principle:
S_d -R- S_r

Thorndike's theory about the importance of developing a strong bond between situation and response was continued and extended by B. F. Skinner at Harvard University. The basic principle of Skinner's operant conditioning theory is that a specific stimulus is given to produce a response, and then a reinforcing stimulus is provided as feedback.

By applying this principle to teaching, we see instruction as a set of discriminating stimuli (S_d) that produces desirable learner responses (R). The emphasis is not just on what instruction provides to learners (S_d), but on what the learners need to accomplish (R)—that is, the learning outcomes. When a learner response is produced, a reinforcing stimulus (S_r) is given to the learner in order to increase (or decrease) the likelihood of the desirable (or undesirable) response occurring again. Skinner's work helped to shift the focus in education from the instructor's behavior (S) to the learner's overt behavior (R).

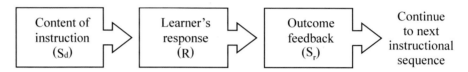

Figure 8. An instructional sequence based on behavioral learning principles.

Skinner's operant conditioning theory has become the foundation for the design of a systematic instructional structure, such as identifying behavior to be changed, formulating a systematic sequence of stimuli, selecting effective reinforcement, and scheduling the reinforcement. Skinner (1968) described teaching as "an arrangement of contingencies of reinforcement under which behavior changes" (p. 113), and explained *a technology of teaching* as not just the teaching machine that displays the arrangement of the contingencies of reinforcement, but also as many kinds of "programming" (i.e., design) of the contingencies of reinforcement.

Programmed
instruction

An early form of programmed instruction was developed by Sydney L. Pressey, a psychologist at Ohio State University in the 1920s. The programmed instruction movement was further promoted by Skinner's theory and research (Saettler, 1968).

Programmed instruction is a learning environment that is
• prescribed;
• individualized; and
• outcome oriented.

The content, sequence, and feedback used in programmed instruction are prescribed. Programmed instruction presents new instructional content to learners in a controlled sequence. Individual learners work through the program by themselves at their own speed. After each module, their learning outcomes are tested and immediate feedback is provided.

An example of programmed instruction

Figure 9 depicts one of Skinner's examples of programmed instruction. This set of frames is designed to teach third- and fourth-grade students to spell the word *manufacture*.

---

1. **Manufacture** means to make or build. *Chair factories manufacture chairs.* Copy the word here:

    — — — — — — — — — — — —

2. Part of the word is like part of the word **factory**. Both parts come from an old word meaning *make* or *build*.

    m a n u __ __ __ __ u r e

3. Part of the word is like part of the word **manual**. Both parts come from an old word for *hand*. Many things are made by hand.

    __ __ __ __ f a c t u r e

4. The same letter goes in both spaces.

    m __ n u f __ c t u r e

5. The same letter goes in both spaces.

    m a n __ f a c t __ r e

6. **Chair factories** __ __ __ __ __ __ __ __ __ __ __ **chairs**.

Figure 9. "A set of frames designed to teach a third- or fourth-grade pupil to spell the word *manufacture*" (Skinner, 1958, p. 972).

An example
of self-paced
instruction
(Letourneau,
2007)

Let's look at an example of self-paced instruction using the principles of programmed instruction.

Topic: Basic Life-Support Skills

Objective: To be able to identify three immediate actions to perform if you see an adult who seems to be seriously ill

---

Start Here

Responding to any kind of emergency can be a very scary experience. Preparing yourself for that situation is one way to make it a little less scary.

This is a brief review of three specific actions you should take if you come upon an adult who seems to be seriously ill. Read the information presented and follow the instructions to work your way through this module.

Imagine yourself at an airport waiting in line to check your luggage. A man about 50 to 60 years old behind you looks like he is about to faint. His traveling companion helps to lower him to the floor. Would you know what to do?

Before providing any assistance, the first thing you should do is to make sure the environment is safe. In this case, is there water on the floor? Do you need to remove additional luggage from around the man in order to get to him? It will only take a few seconds of your time to make a quick assessment to see if the floor area is safe.

In this situation, what would you do? Choose one of the two answers below, and then proceed to the page indicated.

Your Answer	Page to Select
1. I would move any extra luggage from around the man and be sure the floor area around him is clear and dry.	If you picked answer #1, continue to **Page B.**
2. I would jump on top of the luggage to get to the man, and try to talk to him while standing on top of the luggage.	If you picked answer #2, continue to **Page A.**

Page A

You answered, "I would jump on top of the luggage to get to the man, and try to talk to him while standing on top of the luggage."

This answer is not correct.

It is important for you to be sure that the scene is safe before you try to assist someone who might be seriously ill. Moving the luggage and making sure that the area around the man is clear and dry are prudent measures to take. Not only do you want to be sure that you have a safe area in which to work, but you also want to be sure that you are not injured as well.

Please go back to **Start Here**. Re-read the information and answer the question again.

Page B

You answered, "I would move any extra luggage from around the man and be sure the floor area around him is clear and dry."

This is the correct answer.

You want to make sure that the area where the man is located is safe for you to continue helping him, and you must also be sure that you are not in any danger.

Continue to **Page C**.

Page C

Now that you are sure that the scene is safe, you need to position the man on his back and try to get a response from him.

Gently move him so that he is lying on his back and on a firm, flat surface. Since he is on the floor already, this should only take a few seconds.

Kneel beside the man and tap his shoulders with your hands. Shout loud enough into his ear to see if he makes any kind of response. By doing this, you are determining the man's responsiveness.

At this point, you have made sure that the scene is safe and now you are assessing whether or not the man is responsive. Select the action you will take from the two choices below that best describes how to determine if the man is responsive.

Choose one of the two answers below, and then proceed to the page indicated.

Your Answer	Page to Select
1. I would try to remove the man's coat and tie so that I can see if he is breathing.	If you picked answer #1, continue to **Page D.**
2. I would shake the man's shoulders and shout loud enough into his ear to see if he responds.	If you picked answer #2, continue to **Page E.**

Page D

You answered, "I would try to remove the man's coat and tie so that I can see if he is breathing."

This answer is incorrect.

The best way to determine if the man is able to respond to you is by tapping his shoulders and shouting, "Are you okay?" loud enough for him to hear you.

Return to **Page C** to review the information and answer the question again.

Page E

You answered, "I would shake the man's shoulders and shout loud enough into his ear to see if he responds."

This answer is correct.

You must determine whether or not the man is able to respond to you before you know what you do next. If he responds, you can assist him as needed. However, if he doesn't respond, you will need to perform the third action.

Proceed to **Page F**.

Page F

Let's do a quick recap here. You made sure that the scene was safe, and then you determined that the man was not able to respond to you.

The third action you must take is to telephone the emergency response number and get ahold of an automated external defibrillator (AED).

In most public places, the emergency response number is 911. (*Note:* Some work settings have a different number to call. Be sure you know what number to call in your work area.) Once you have determined that the man is not responsive, ask someone nearby to find a telephone and dial 911 to request medical assistance. If an AED is available, that person should return to you with the AED.

If no one else is around, you need to leave the man immediately and call the emergency response number yourself. This might seem awkward, but it is most important to get help on the way as soon as possible.

Now, back to the airport situation. The man behind you in line is on the floor. The scene is safe and you determined that he is unresponsive. What would you do next?

Choose one of the two answers below, and then proceed to the page indicated.

Your Answer	Page to Select
1. I would tell someone nearby to call 911 for medical assistance, get ahold of an AED if there is one, and come back to me.	If you picked answer #1, continue to **Page G.**
2. I would try to remove the man's coat and tie to make sure he can breathe.	If you picked answer #2, continue to **Page H.**

Page G

You answered, "I would tell someone nearby to call 911 for medical assistance, get ahold of an AED if there is one, and come back to me."

You are correct!

Getting help on the way is of utmost importance. And remember, if you are by yourself, you must leave the man and call 911 yourself. You must get the AED if there is one, and then return to the man.

Continue on to **Page I**.

Page H

You answered, "I would try to remove the man's coat and tie to make sure he can breathe."

This answer is incorrect.

Getting help on the way as soon as possible is of utmost importance. The sooner you get an emergency medical services team to help the man, the better his chances.

Please continue on to **Page F**. Reread the information and answer the question again.

Page I

Congratulations! You now know the three immediate actions to take if you see an adult who seems to be seriously ill. Let's review them one more time:

1. Make sure that the surrounding area is safe.
2. Check for response by tapping the person and shouting.
3. Try to get help by phoning the emergency response number (usually 911).

What do you do next?

The next step is to begin performing CPR (cardiopulmonary resuscitation). To learn these skills, please contact your local American Heart Association office to find a class near you. Their Web site is http://www.americanheart.org.

Knowing what to do in case of an emergency is a great skill to have. If you forget, the best thing you can do is to call your emergency response number. The staff on the other end of the phone will provide you with all the information you need, and keep you calm at the same time.

The End

The overall flow of this programmed instruction is a series of S_d (instructional content), R (learner response; correct or wrong), and S_r (feedback), as shown in Figure 10. This type of self-paced instruction can be presented in a booklet or via a computer program. Many of the current self-paced e-learning programs use instructional sequences that have evolved from the programmed instruction.

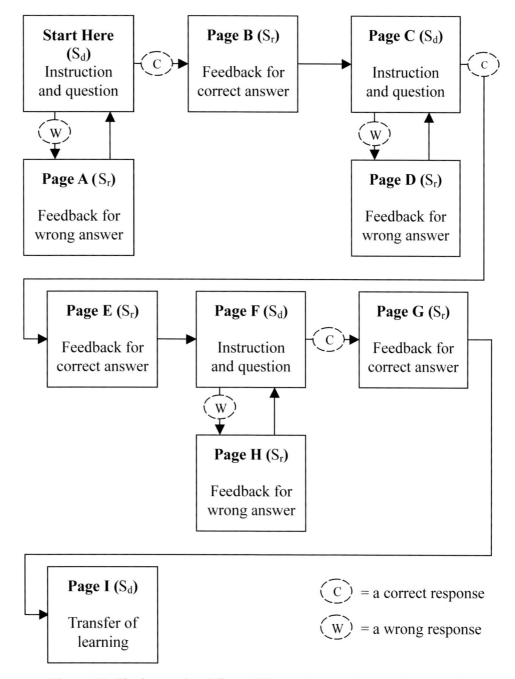

Figure 10. The instructional flow of the programmed instruction example.

Benjamin Samuel Bloom (1913–1999)

Influence of Tyler's work	Just as Ralph Tyler was influenced by the work of E. L. Thorndike, Benjamin Bloom had Ralph Tyler as a mentor after they met at the University of Chicago. Bloom worked with Tyler in the university examiner's office. Tyler directed Bloom's attention to the development of a system or specification to be used to categorize educational objectives according to their complexity (Eisner, 2000).
Taxonomy of educational objectives	Bloom and his colleagues developed a taxonomy of educational objectives through a series of meetings held from 1949 to 1953 in order to "provide for classification of the goals of our educational system" (Bloom, Engelhart, Furst, Hill, & Krathwohl, 1956, p. 1). The original idea of developing a theoretical framework for a classification system came from a group of college examiners who needed a communication system so that they could share testing-related information with one another. Their shared belief that evaluation criteria and testing materials should be developed based on well-defined educational objectives led them to conclude that such a classification system would be obtained by developing a taxonomy of educational objectives. Bloom and his colleagues preferred the term *taxonomy* to synonyms such as *classification* in order to emphasize the hierarchical order of the categories.
Three domains of the taxonomy	Bloom and his colleagues defined three domains in the taxonomy of educational objectives: (1) cognitive domain, (2) affective domain, and (3) psychomotor domain, as can be seen in Table 4.

Table 4. Three Domains of the Taxonomy of Educational Objectives

Cognitive Domain	Affective Domain	Psychomotor Domain

• A classification of objectives that improve learners' intellectual abilities
 	
• Six levels:
  1. Knowledge
  2. Comprehension
  3. Application
  4. Analysis
  5. Synthesis
  6. Evaluation
	• A classification of objectives that focus on the development of emotions, values, and attitudes
	
	• Five levels:
	  1. Receiving
	  2. Responding
	  3. Valuing
	  4. Organization
	  5. Characterization by a value or value complex
		A classification of objectives about muscular movements, manipulation of objects, or acts that require bodily coordination

Values of the taxonomy	Bloom and his colleagues saw the following values for creating a classification scheme (Krathwohl, Bloom, & Masia, 1964):

1. It helps clarify the language of objectives; use clear and meaningful statements of objectives; and avoid meaningless clichés.

2. It provides a reliable system for describing test items or evaluation instruments. In other words, test materials are developed based on objectives and contents.

3. It allows comparing and studying the effectiveness of instructional programs with similar objectives.

4. Once the hierarchical order of the outcomes in each domain is confirmed by observations and research studies, it will facilitate the development of a new theory of learning and instruction.

The cognitive domain	Since cognitive development was the major emphasis in the secondary and college level, Bloom and his colleagues considered the cognitive domain as the top priority and published the first handbook for the cognitive domain of the taxonomy of educational objectives in 1956. Bloom was the first author of the handbook, and for that reason, Bloom's *taxonomy of educational objectives* often implies the cognitive domain section. Here are definitions of the six levels of the cognitive domain (Bloom, Engelhart, Furst, Hill, & Krathwohl, 1956):

1. **Knowledge.** "The recall of specific and isolable bits of information" (p. 63). Using a file cabinet as an analogy, the knowledge level is about remembering if a certain piece of information is stored in a file cabinet, and if so, in which folder the information is stored.

2. **Comprehension.** "To know what is being communicated and to be able to make some use of the material or ideas contained in it" (p. 89). Three types of comprehension behavior are translation, interpretation, and extrapolation.

3. **Application.** "The use of abstractions in particular and concrete situations" (p. 205). The abstractions include general ideas, principles, rules, theories, models, methods, and procedures. Application-level objectives aim to facilitate "transfer of training."

4. **Analysis.** "The breakdown of the material into its constituent parts and detection of the relationships of the parts and of the way they are organized" (p. 144). Three types of analyses are classification of elements, identifying relationships, and recognition of organizational principles.

5. **Synthesis.** "The putting together of elements and parts so as to form a whole" (p. 162). Learners bring together relevant elements from different sources and put them into a new structure.

6. **Evaluation.** "The making of judgments about the value, for some purpose, of ideas, works, solutions, methods, material, etc. It involves the

use of criteria as well as standards for appraising the extent to which particulars are accurate, effective, economical, or satisfying" (p. 185). One difference between analysis and evaluation is that evaluation includes the use of value-based criteria.

About 40 years after the publication of the first handbook, a group of scholars (including Krathwohl, one of the authors of the handbook on the affective domain) felt a need to incorporate new knowledge in curriculum design into the original taxonomy. They revised it and put it into a two-dimensional structure: The cognitive process dimension (remember, understand, apply, analyze, evaluate, and create), and the knowledge dimension (factual, conceptual, procedural, and meta-cognitive) (Anderson & Krathwohl, 2001).

The affective domain

Bloom and his colleagues also published the second handbook for the affective domain of the taxonomy of educational objectives in 1964 (Krathwohl was its first author). The affective domain emphasizes the change of feelings, interests, emotions, attitudes, appreciations, and values. It contains five levels:

1. **Receiving.** It involves levels of awareness, willingness to receive, and controlled and selected attention to a given stimulus (e.g., develop awareness for maintaining a drug-free workplace).

2. **Responding.** Upon receiving a stimulus, the learner responds to the stimulus through levels of acquiescence in responding, willingness to respond, and satisfaction in response (e.g., being willing to comply with safety rules).

3. **Valuing.** Responding to a stimulus leads to internalization of the information, which involves acceptance of a value, preference for a value, and commitment (e.g., develop responsibility for following health regulations).

4. **Organization.** After perceiving the value of a given stimulus, the learner starts organizing the information, which involves conceptualization of a value and organization of a value system (e.g., formulate ethical standards for professional practice).

5. **Characterization by a value or value complex.** After the internalization and organizational processes, the learner responds to value-driven situations in a consistent manner (e.g., acts consistently based on a philosophy of life).

Bloom and his colleagues did not publish a handbook for the psychomotor domain at that time. Several versions were later published by others (e.g., Simpson, 1972; Harrow, 1972).

Maintaining the hierarchy and congruence	Bloom's taxonomy of educational objectives helps instructional designers construct instructional sequences or strategies in a consistent manner, as presented in Table 5.

Table 5. Application of Bloom's Taxonomy of Educational Objectives

Objectives	Instructional Activities	Assessment Methods
Instructional designers design a series of *objectives* to teach learners complex cognitive skills (such as synthesizing interrelated information) after teaching simpler cognitive skills (such as understanding concepts and principles), which would build on even more simple cognitive skills (such as remembering specific facts).	Instructional designers develop *instructional activities* that help learners achieve the series of pre-set objectives.	Instructional designers develop *assessment methods* that measure the achievement of the series of pre-set objectives.

By using Bloom's taxonomy, instructional designers will not only be able to build a **hierarchical** structure of instructional sequence, but also ensure that there will be **congruence** among the objectives, the instructional activities, and the assessment methods. Bloom's taxonomy of educational objectives can be used for the design of both classroom instruction and online instruction (e.g., Chyung & Stepich, 2003).

Bloom's taxonomy in action	What follows here is a hypothetical instructional design situation illustrating the use of Bloom's taxonomy of educational objectives (cognitive domain).

The Situation: A company recently changed its performance management system from the previous two-level (pass/fail) rating system to a four-level rating system (1 = exemplary, 2 = exceeded expectations, 3 = achieved performance standards, and 4 = did not achieve performance standards). All supervisors at the company are now required to complete training in how to use the new performance management system. The stated instructional goal is that learners will be able to correctly use the new four-level rating system to evaluate the performance of classified staff. The instructional structure in Table 6 was developed in order to provide a step-by-step, hierarchical sequence of instruction from the knowledge level to the evaluation level, and to achieve congruence among the objectives, the instructional activities, and the assessment methods in each level. |

Table 6. An Example of an Instructional Structure

Levels and Objectives	Instructional Activities	Assessment Methods
Knowledge: Learners will list four-level rating categories in the correct order.	• Ask about the previous two-level rating categories that learners are familiar with. • Present the new four-level rating categories with definitions in order (from "exemplary" to "did not achieve performance standards").	In the final test, a rank-order question will be used to measure learner understanding about the correct sequence of the four-level rating categories.
Comprehension: Learners will identify the differences among the four-level rating categories.	• Show examples of measured performance outcomes using the previous two-level rating categories, and compare them to examples of performance outcomes using the new four-level rating categories. • Explain the differences among the new four-level rating categories.	Multiple choice questions will be used in the final test to measure learner understanding about the meaning of each of the four-level rating categories.
Application: Based on hypothetical descriptions of a performance and using an evaluation template form, learners will select an appropriate performance rating for the performance.	• Show a new performance evaluation template. Have learners compare the new template to the previous one, and recognize the changed sections. • Divide the class into several small groups (four to five members in each group). • Provide descriptions of a different hypothetical performance to each group. • Have groups analyze the quality of the performance, and discuss what would be an appropriate performance rating for the performance. • Have individual learners fill out the evaluation form by selecting a proper performance rating and inserting narrative comments.	A scenario-based question will be included in the final test. Learners will analyze the quality of performance presented in the scenario, and select the most appropriate performance rating for the performance.

(continued)

Table 6. An Example of an Instructional Structure *(concluded)*

Levels and Objectives	Instructional Activities	Assessment Methods
Analysis: Given examples of performance ratings and narrative comments, learners will decide whether or not the selection of the performance ratings and the narrative comments were appropriate.	• Give each group an evaluation form completed by another group during the previous activity. • Have each group analyze another group's selection of performance ratings and review narrative comments. • Repeat this activity so that each group has a chance to analyze all other groups' results.	A scenario-based question will be included in the final test. A worker's performance and the performance evaluation form that he or she received will be described. Learners will analyze and determine if the performance was appropriately evaluated.
Synthesis: Based on examples of fair and unfair performance evalua-tions (including incon-sistent ones), learners will develop a list of guidelines that supervisors should follow.	• Present examples of fair and unfair, and consistent and inconsistent evaluations. • Divide the class into small groups, and have them generate a list of guidelines. • Have the groups share their guidelines.	A scenario-based question will be used in the final test to measure learner understanding about the principles of fair vs. unfair, and consistent vs. inconsistent performance evaluations.
Evaluation: Learners will identify the benefits of using the four-level rating categories, in terms of ensuring fairness and consistency in perform-ance evaluations.	• Provide examples of performance evaluations that were administered in an inconsistent manner. • Discuss the differences between the two-level categories and the four-level categories in terms of ensuring fairness.	A scenario-based question will be used in the final test to measure learner understanding about the problems associated with inconsistent evaluations and the benefits of using the four-level rating categories.

References

Aikin, W. M. (1942). *Adventures in American education. Volume I: The story of the Eight-Year Study*. New York: Harper and Brothers.

Anderson, L. W., & Krathwohl, D. R. (2001). *A taxonomy for learning, teaching, and assessing: A revision of Bloom's taxonomy of educational objectives* (Complete edition). New York: Addison Wesley Longman, Inc.

Bloom, B. S., Engelhart, M. D., Furst, E. J., Hill, W. H., & Krathwohl, D. R. (1956). *Taxonomy of educational objectives: The classification of educational goals (Handbook I: Cognitive domain)*. New York: David McKay Company, Inc.

Chyung, S. Y., & Stepich, D. (2003). Applying the "congruence" principle of Bloom's Taxonomy to designing online instruction. *Quarterly Review of Distance Education, 4*(3), 317–330.

Eisner, E. (2000). *Benjamin Bloom: 1913–99*. Retrieved August 27, 2004, from http://www.ibe.unesco.org/Publications/ThinkersPdf/bloome.pdf

Harrow, A. (1972). *A taxonomy of the psychomotor domain: A guide for developing behavioral objectives*. New York: David McKay Company, Inc.

Krathwohl, D. R., Bloom, B. S., & Masia, B. B. (1964). *Taxonomy of educational objectives: The classification of educational goals (Handbook II: Affective domain)*. New York: David McKay Company, Inc.

Letourneau, J. (2007). *An example of self-paced programmed instruction*. Unpublished manuscript at Boise State University.

Saettler, P. (1968). *A history of instructional technology*. New York: McGraw-Hill.

Saettler, P. (1990). *The evolution of American educational technology*. Englewood, CO: Libraries Unlimited, Inc.

Scriven, M. (1967). The methodology of evaluation. In O. Smith (Ed.), *Perspectives of curriculum evaluation: AERA monograph series on curriculum evaluation No. 1* (pp. 39–83). Chicago: Rand McNally & Company.

Simpson, E. (1972). *The classification of educational objectives in the psychomotor domain: The psychomotor domain* (Vol. 3). Washington, DC: Gryphon House.

Skinner, B. F. (1958). Teaching machines. *Science, 128* (3330), 969–977.

Skinner, B. F. (1968). *The technology of teaching*. New York: Appleton-Century-Crofts.

Smith, E. R., Tyler, R. W., & the Evaluation Staff (1942). *Adventures in American education. Volume III: Appraising and recording student progress*. New York: Harper and Brothers.

Thorndike, E. L. (1906). *The principles of teaching*. New York: A. G. Seiler.

Thorndike, E. L. (1912). *Education, a first book*. New York: The Macmillan Company.

Thorndike, E. L., & Gates, A. I. (1929). *Elementary principles of education*. New York: The Macmillan Company.

Tyler, R. W. (1949). *Basic principles of curriculum and instruction*. Chicago: The University of Chicago Press.

Tyler, R. W. (1976). Two new emphases in curriculum development. *Educational Leadership, 34*(1), 61–71.

Tyler, R. W. (1981). Curriculum development since 1900. *Educational Leadership, 38*(8), 598–601.

Tyler, R. W. (1986/1987). The five most significant curriculum events in the twentieth century. *Educational Leadership, 44*(4), 36–38.

Systematic Instructional Design

The Systematic Process of Instructional Design

Theories vs. models	**the·o·ry** \ˈthē-ə-rē, ˈthir-ē\ *n, pl* **-ries** — a plausible or scientifically acceptable general principle or body of principles offered to explain phenomena — a hypothesis assumed for the sake of argument or investigation — an unproved assumption — a body of theorems presenting a concise systematic view of a subject (Merriam-Webster's Collegiate Dictionary, 2003, p. 1296) **mod·el** \ˈmä-dᵊl\ *n* — a description or analogy used to help visualize something (as an atom) that cannot be directly observed — a system of postulates, data, and inferences presented as a mathematical description of an entity or state of affairs (Merriam-Webster's Collegiate Dictionary, 2003, p. 798)
Development of instructional theories and design models	The field of instructional design provides "a theoretical foundation to principles of instructional design, a research base confirming the theoretical foundations, and a direct involvement in the application of those principles" (Tennyson & Schott, 1997). Instructional design as a field of study started gaining recognition during the 1950s and 1960s when a lot of instructional theories and models were developed. The early development of the field of instructional design was led by the work of pioneers such as Robert Gagné, Robert Mager, David Ausubel, and Jerome Bruner. While the applications of behaviorism to teaching and learning were waning in the late 1960s and throughout the 1970s, cognitivism gained popularity. In the 1990s, constructivist theories also started to influence the development of new instructional approaches.
Systematic guidance	Instructional design models provide instructional designers with guidance in systematic instructional design and help them improve the probability that desired learning will occur due to the instruction they designed. Instructional design models help instructional designers be aware of all the interdependent elements in the instructional system (e.g., learners, media, methods, materials, learning environments, etc.) and be able to use the most appropriate combination of those elements. With the guidance of instructional design models, instructional designers will be able to produce reliable and desired outcomes of learning.
Systems approaches to instructional design	This chapter provides an overview of various individual contributions to the development of instructional theories and systematic instructional design processes, including those of Robert Gagné, Robert Mager, Walter Dick and Lou Carey, and John Keller.

Robert Gagné's Instructional Theories

Robert M.
Gagné
(1916–2002)

Robert Gagné received a Ph.D. in experimental psychology from Brown University. He served as a director of research of the American Institutes for Research and pursued his academic career at Princeton University, the University of California–Berkeley, and Florida State University (Gagné & Medsker, 1996). Robert Gagné is well known for developing instructional theories about learning hierarchies, domains and conditions of learning, and the nine events of instruction.

His main interest was in applying knowledge obtained from experimental psychology to actual instructional design. "How can what you know about learning as an event, or as a process, be put to use in designing training so that it will be maximally effective?" (Gagné, 1962, p. 84).

Gagné was a prolific writer. His published works cover six decades, starting in the late 1930s. He made great contributions to the development of instructional theory and design practice in the fields of education and military training (see Richey, 2000).

The domains
and conditions
of learning

Gagné published four editions of his book *The Conditions of Learning* (1965, 1970, 1977, 1985), and another edition of the book on training applications in 1996. After several revisions of his theory on different types of learning, in the third edition of the book, published in 1977, Gagné finally defined the five major types of learning outcomes that learners are capable of achieving:

1. Verbal information: declarative knowledge (knowing that)
2. Intellectual skills: procedural knowledge (knowing how)
3. Cognitive strategies: strategic knowledge (self-management skills)
4. Attitudes: a belief, emotion, or action that influences behavior
5. Motor skills: physical movement

Gagné (1988) emphasized that it is important to categorize learning outcomes, because the types of learning capabilities require different optimal conditions in instruction.

For example, the process for learning verbal information would be quite different from that of attitudes. Instructional conditions needed for verbal information would focus on the process of meaningful encoding, storage, and retrieval using distinctive cues and practice, whereas human modeling might be an appropriate condition for changing attitudes (Gagné, 1977).

Figure 11 illustrates the different conditions of learning provided by external events of instruction to produce different domains of learning outcomes.

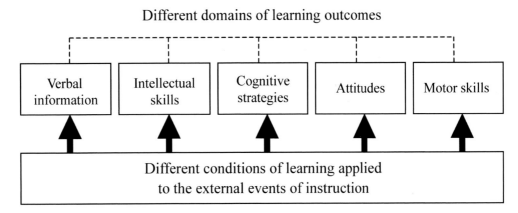

Figure 11. Gagné's theories on domains and conditions of learning.

As shown in Table 7, Gagné's five types of learning outcomes are similar to the three domains of taxonomy that Bloom and his colleagues classified. Verbal information, intellectual skills, and cognitive strategies can be grouped into the cognitive domain; attitudes parallel the affective domain; and motor skills parallel the psychomotor domain.

Table 7.   Bloom and his Colleagues' Three Domains of Taxonomy
vs. Gagné's Five Domains of Learning Outcomes

Three Domains of Taxonomy	Five Domains of Learning Outcomes
Cognitive domain	• Verbal information
	• Intellectual skills
	• Cognitive strategies
Affective domain	Attitudes
Psychomotor domain	Motor skills

The nine events of instruction

Gagné formulated his idea of events of instruction in the late 1960s, basing it on two sources: empirical observations of instructional procedures and the information-processing model of human learning and memory. He believed that learning involves a sequence of steps to transform information and that instruction should be a set of external events that influences or supports the internal processes of learning. This belief was based particularly on the information-processing model (Gagné, 1988).

As he did for his other instructional theories, Gagné continued to refine his idea of external events of instruction in the 1960s and 1970s (see Gagné, 1965, 1970). For example, his early theory of the external events of instruction was described as:

a. employ techniques to gain and maintain the attention of the learner;
b. establish within the learner certain preconditions for learning by giving pretraining, by providing verbal directions, by stimulating recall;
c. present the stimuli directly involved in learning as actual objects and events, printed materials, or pictures, among other forms;
d. aid the learning process by methods of prompting and guiding, often in the form of verbal communications;
e. specify the conditions for responding as in the contrast between overt and covert responses;
f. employ methods to provide feedback to the learner concerning the correctness of his performance at various stages of learning;
g. establish conditions to promote retention, including such factors as repetition and rehearsal;
h. use techniques which enhance the transfer of learning to subsequent learning tasks or other performances (Gagné & Rohwer, 1969, p. 382).

Then the final form of the nine events of instruction appeared in the fourth edition of *The Conditions of Learning*, which was published in 1985:

1. Gain attention
2. Inform learner of the objective
3. Stimulate recall of prior knowledge (relevant prerequisites)
4. Present new content
5. Provide learning guidance
6. Elicit performance
7. Provide feedback
8. Assess performance
9. Enhance retention and transfer (Gagné, 1985, pp. 302–330)

The nine events do not always have to be followed in the exact order, and some steps may be omitted depending on the situation (Gagné, 1970, 1988; Gagné & Medsker, 1996). For example:

• Learners' attention can be gained by presenting learning objectives in an interesting way (i.e., combining Events #1 and #2).
• Learners can be asked to recall prior knowledge before they are informed of new objectives (i.e., presenting Event #3 before Event #2).
• New content can be successfully presented without stimulating recall of any particular prior knowledge (i.e., omitting Event #3).
• Instead of providing feedback after learners complete their practice, feedback can be provided during the process of practicing performance (i.e., combining Events #6 and #7).
• Learners' performance on multiple lessons can be assessed together at the end of the course (i.e., moving Event #8 from a lesson-level assessment to a course-level assessment).

Robert Mager's Method of Preparing Instructional Objectives

Behavioral objectives, instructional objectives, and learning objectives

E. L. Thorndike is credited with promoting the importance of establishing *educational aims*, and Ralph Tyler is credited as the one who used the term *behavioral objectives* to advocate that objectives should be written in terms of learners' behavioral outcomes. Robert Mager, however, is credited with educating practitioners in how to write behavioral objectives. Mager published his book *Preparing Objectives for Programmed Instruction* in 1961, but he changed its title slightly in 1962 to *Preparing Instructional Objectives* because he realized that his method could be applied to more than just programmed instruction (Heinich, Molenda, Russell, & Smaldino, 1999). Subsequent editions were published in 1975 and 1997.

There are two synonyms for behavioral objectives: *instructional objectives* and *learning objectives*. All of these terms refer to the status of learning outcomes to be accomplished at the end of instruction. They are written in terms of what learners will be able to do after successfully completing the instruction, instead of what the instructor or learners will be doing during instructional and learning processes. For instance, the first example below is appropriately written as an instructional objective, but the other examples are not:

1. Students will correctly point out the performance problem, given the descriptions of the situation. (Note: This statement indicates what learners will be able to do if they have successfully completed the instruction.)
2. The instructor will use a role play to encourage students' participation while learning. (Note: This statement indicates what the instructor will be doing during instruction.)
3. Students will work on 10 math problems. (Note: This statement indicates what learners will be doing during the learning process.)

Methods for writing instructional objectives

Mager's method of writing instructional objectives consists of three elements:

• Performance (What is the learner expected to be able to do?)
• Conditions (Under what conditions will the performance occur?)
• Criterion (What is the level of competence that should be attained?)

Here is the instructional objective that Mager wrote for his book *Preparing Instructional Objectives* (1997), using his own method:

> Given any objective in a subject area with which you are familiar, be able to identify (label) correctly the *performance*, the *conditions*, and the *criteria* of acceptable performance when those characteristics are present. (p. vii)

In this objective, the performance is to "identify (label) the *performance*, the *conditions*, and the *criteria* of acceptable performance when those characteristics are present." The condition is "given any objective in a subject area with which you are familiar." The criterion is "correctly."

The ABCD Method is similar to Mager's method (Heinich, Molenda, & Russell, 1989):

- Audience (Who is the learner?)
- Behavior (What will the learner be able to do at the end of instruction?)
- Conditions (Under what conditions will the behavior be observed?)
- Degree (How accurately should the learner complete it?)

The two methods contain the same elements for writing instructional objectives, except that the audience indicator is not included in Mager's method (see Table 8).

Table 8. The ABCD Method vs. Mager's Method for Writing Objectives

The ABCD Method	Mager's Method
Audience	(not included or assumed)
Behavior	Performance
Conditions	Conditions
Degree	Criterion

As Tyler emphasized during the Eight-Year Study, a widely accepted principle in writing instructional objectives is to use action verbs to clearly indicate the planned behavior or performance. Action verbs are the words that indicate overt behaviors that can be observed. They help instructional designers communicate their intent to the users of the instructional objectives including the instructors and learners. Not using action verbs can lead to misinterpretation of the objectives (Mager, 1997).

For example, the meaning of the performance indicator *to know* is open to interpretation, whereas the performance indicator *to identify* is specific and measurable.

Here are examples of action verbs: *select, move, run, construct, build, compare, contrast, solve, add, write, indicate, circle, underline,* and *demonstrate.*

A sample
lesson plan
(Berg, 2007)

Table 9 presents an example of a lesson designed with Gagné's nine events of instruction. The lesson objective is written based on Mager's method. In this example, the step for gaining attention and the step for stimulating recall of prior knowledge were combined into one step and presented up front. The step of eliciting performance and the step of providing feedback were also combined, as the two instructional steps occur simultaneously.

Background: Bulgarian workers have been hired by an international firm for English-speaking positions as international tax specialists. Most of the firm's clients are North American or Western European. The job requires frequent phone communication, but the new employees are not familiar with the concept of "good customer service" as defined by the mainstream culture of their clients. The new hires are working on commission and are highly motivated to learn how to better communicate with clients by phone.

Lesson objective: Given the opportunity to make practice calls, newly hired international tax specialists will provide good telephone customer service that North American and Western European clients expect to receive by phone.

Media and materials to be used: A flipchart, a cassette tape player, and an audiotape.

Table 9. A Sample Lesson Plan

Events of Instruction	Planned Instructional Activities	Anticipated Learner Activities
Gain attention and stimulate recall of prior knowledge	• The instructor asks a couple of volunteers in the group to share a positive experience that they had at a store or restaurant, where the quality of that experience was influenced by an employee of that business. • The instructor then asks for volunteers to share a negative experience of this nature. • While participants are describing their experience, the instructor writes key words from each on a flipchart. After each person has had a turn, the instructor leads a discussion on what the employee did in each situation to deliver good or bad service.	• Participants tell stories based on their experiences. • Participants listen to the stories, making note of the key points the instructor is writing on the flipchart. • Participants then discuss the actions taken by the employee in each situation that made the experience a positive or negative one for the patron. • Participants actively engage in the discussion, and use their experiences to distinguish between poor service and good service.

(continued)

Table 9. A Sample Lesson Plan *(continued)*

Events of Instruction	Planned Instructional Activities	Anticipated Learner Activities
Inform learners of objective	The instructor introduces the purpose of the lesson and explains how this lesson will help participants better communicate with their clients and prevent incidents in which their clients feel dissatisfied with the service, which might lead to their decision to leave the organization.	As new employees working on commission, the participants relate the objective to the earlier discussion and are motivated to learn about the clients' expectations of customer service in order to maintain positive client relationships.
Present new content	• The instructor defines "customer service" and presents the characteristics of good and poor customer service, integrating the participants' responses from the previous activity into the discussion. • The instructor explains expectations that the clients are likely to have regarding customer service. • The instructor asks participants to compare clients' expectations to theirs.	• Participants relate the new information to their own experiences. As a result, participants are able to gain a clear understanding of how customer service is defined and the types of actions that the clients expect when receiving service. • Participants explain how the clients' expectations are different from what they are familiar with.
Provide learning guidance	The instructor plays a recording of a phone conversation with a client in which elements of poor customer service are present. The instructor also asks which part of the call should be improved and how.	Participants apply their newly learned principles to the recorded phone call to identify areas of improvement and suggest how those areas could be better handled.
Elicit performance and provide feedback	• The instructor pairs up participants to engage in a role-play exercise—one person acts the part of a customer and the other plays a tax examiner. • The instructor asks participants to provide feedback on the customer service rendered.	• Participants use the principles in a role-play exercise. • They also refer to these principles when providing feedback to their partners. • Participants identify their strengths and areas needing improvement in delivering customer service.

(continued)

Table 9. A Sample Lesson Plan *(concluded)*

Events of Instruction	Planned Instructional Activities	Anticipated Learner Activities
Elicit performance and provide feedback *(concluded)*	• The instructor leads a discussion about the role-play exercise, asking participants to discuss which situations were easy to handle and which were more difficult. • The instructor encourages other participants in the group to give one another feedback.	They also evaluate the comments of their peers, based on the principles they have learned and offer advice.
Assess performance	The instructor asks participants to practice making service calls with their supervisors and trainers until they have met all specified criteria.	• Participants practice service calls with their supervisors and trainers, as though they were real. • Supervisors and trainers provide feedback to participants after the calls. Participants make reflective comments on their performance.
Enhance retention and transfer	• The instructor provides a checklist of customer service basics. • After training, the participants start taking live calls with clients.	Participants continue to receive feedback on their live calls with clients from supervisors after the training is complete to ensure that the customer service principles are applied correctly.

Dick and Carey's Model of Instructional Design

A systematic
approach to
instructional
design

It was about three decades ago when Walter Dick, a professor at Florida State University, and Lou Carey, a doctoral student, developed the systematic instructional design model while preparing to teach a graduate course titled *Techniques of Programmed Instruction* (Dick, 1997). The model was published in the first edition of the book *The Systematic Design of Instruction* in 1978.

Dick and Carey (1996) define a system as "a set of interrelated parts, all of which work together toward a defined goal" (p. 3). Both the instructional process and the instructional design process can be viewed as a procedural system in which the input, output, and feedback mechanisms should work together to reach and maintain the goal. Dick and Carey's instructional design model is thus a *systematic* instructional design model that also provides a *systemic* perspective: it takes a comprehensive view of instructional design in that various components of the instructional system (such as the instructor, the learners, the instructional materials, and the learning environment) interact with one another in order to achieve the instructional goal.

The systematic
instructional
design model

In the context of instructional design, the word *model* usually refers to an organized set of procedures for solving a problem. Models are based on theories and research findings, as well as on experience-based reasoning (Briggs, 1970; Briggs & Wagner, 1981).

The *problem* to be solved in an instructional context is usually one of two things: (a) the existing instruction does not produce desired learning outcomes or (b) there is a need to develop new instruction. The *specific purpose* of using a model in such cases is usually to guide the preparation of an instructional package. To produce predetermined learning outcomes effectively and efficiently, *systematic* approaches should be applied to the design of instruction.

Dick and Carey (1996) explain that they were influenced by the work of Robert Gagné, Leslie Briggs, Robert Mager, Robert Glaser, and Lee Cronbach. For example, Briggs developed a 10-step model for designing instruction in the early 1970s:

1. State objectives and performance standards
2. Prepare tests over the objectives
3. Analyze objectives for structure and sequence
4. Identify assumed entering competencies
5. Prepare pretests and remedial instruction
    or plan an adaptive program
    or screen students or accept drop-outs
    or plan a dual-track program

6. Select media and write prescriptions
7. Develop first-draft materials
8. [Conduct] Small-group tryouts and revisions
9. [Conduct] Classroom tryouts and revisions
10. [Conduct a] Performance evaluation (Briggs, 1970, p. 7)

In contrast (but with some similarity), there are nine steps in Dick and Carey's model of instructional design. Each step has its own input and output, both of which contribute to developing the predetermined instructional product:

1. Identify instructional goal(s).
2. Conduct instructional analysis.
3. Analyze learners and contexts.
4. Write performance objectives.
5. Develop assessment instruments.
6. Develop instructional strategy.
7. Develop and select instructional material.
8. Design and conduct the formative evaluation of instruction.
9. Revise instruction. (Dick, Carey & Carey, 2005, pp. 6–7)

The last step in Dick and Carey's model of instructional design leads into a summative evaluation to measure the value or worth of the instruction. This is external to the instructional design process and is usually conducted by an external evaluator without the involvement of the instructional designer.

Dick and Carey's model of instructional design is a performance-oriented instructional design model that emphasizes the identification of skills to be learned and the use of data obtained from learners for revision of instruction.

However, Dick and Carey's model of instructional design is not an instructional systems development (ISD) model that starts with a (training) needs assessment phase, whose main purpose is to reevaluate the suspected instructional problems to determine their exact nature in terms of the needs of the organization, the learners, and the job (Rosenberg, 1982).

Instead, Dick and Carey's model of instructional design assumes that the needs assessment has already shown that instruction is an appropriate intervention (Dick, 1997). In other words, instructional designers who apply Dick and Carey's model of instructional design should have the outcome of a needs assessment that clearly shows that instruction is needed. They can then proceed with the first step of stating instructional goals.

John Keller's ARCS Model

The ARCS factors

John Keller, a professor at Florida State University, developed the ARCS model in the early 1980s. He based it on the expectancy-value theory, which explains that people tend to be motivated to participate in an activity when

- their personal needs are satisfied (the value of it); and

- they expect a positive result from doing it (the expectancy aspect) (Keller, 1987a).

The ARCS model is based on the theory-based assumption that learners tend to ask themselves various questions that can be grouped into four categories: Attention, Relevance, Confidence, and Satisfaction. For example:

1. **Attention**. What is happening? Is the instruction interesting to me? Is it new to me? Do I like it? Does it stimulate my curiosity? Is it challenging enough?
2. **Relevance**. Is it what I wanted to learn? Does the outcome of learning match my goal? Will I be able to use the knowledge later? Is the environment friendly? Do I feel that I achieved something useful?
3. **Confidence**. Will I be able to learn the material? Will I be able to reach my goal if I do my best, or does it depend on luck? Will I get help if or when I need it?
4. **Satisfaction**. Am I learning? Am I learning something valuable? Do I like the consequences of my successful learning?

Keller (1987b) suggests that in order to help learners become and remain motivated to learn, instructional designers or instructors should design instruction with the following questions in mind to meet the four general categories of requirements (attention, relevance, confidence, and satisfaction):

- How can I make the instruction stimulating and valuable to learners (i.e., attention and relevance)?

- How can I help learners succeed and feel that they are responsible for their success (i.e., confidence and satisfaction)?

Therefore, the ARCS model is "a method for improving the motivational appeal of instructional materials" (Keller, 1987a, p. 2). One can improve the motivational appeal of instruction by considering the four factors during the instructional design processes and by using effective motivational strategies.

| The ARCS strategies | The ARCS model provides a framework for developing motivational strategies by posing questions, as shown in Table 10. |

Table 10. Motivational Categories of the ARCS Model

Categories and Subcategories	Process Questions
Attention A.1. Perceptual Arousal A.2. Inquiry Arousal A.3. Variability	 • What can I do to capture my learners' interest? • How can I stimulate an attitude of inquiry? • How can I maintain my learners' attention?
Relevance R.1. Goal Orientation R.2. Motive Matching R.3. Familiarity	 • How can I best meet my learners' needs? (Do I know their needs?) • How and when can I provide my learners with appropriate choices, responsibilities, and influences? • How can I tie the instruction to learners' experiences?
Confidence C.1. Learning Requirements C.2. Success Opportunities C.3. Personal Control	 • How can I assist in building a positive expectation for success? • How will the learning experience support or enhance my learners' beliefs in their competence? • How will my learners clearly know their success is based on their efforts and abilities?
Satisfaction S.1. Natural Consequences S.2. Positive Consequences S.3. Equity	 • How can I provide meaningful opportunities for my learners to use their newly acquired knowledge/skill? • What will provide reinforcement to the learners' successes? • How can I assist my learners in anchoring a positive feeling about their accomplishments?

Note. From *The Systematic Process of Motivational Design* (p. 2) by J. Keller. Copyright © 1987 by the International Society for Performance Improvement. Reprinted with permission of John Wiley & Sons, Inc.

Systematic process of motivational design

Keller (1987a) also suggests following a systematic process when applying the ARCS model during instructional design:

1. Classify the motivational problem.
2. Conduct audience analysis.
3. Prepare motivational objectives.
4. Generate potential motivational strategies.
5. Select motivational strategies.
6. Develop motivational elements.
7. Integrate motivational strategies into instruction.
8. Conduct developmental try-out.
9. Assess motivational outcomes.

The ARCS model can be used in the design of classroom instruction, but can also be used for online instruction (Chyung, 2001). When applying the ARCS model, instructional designers should not use it as a behavioral modification model. It is not intended to be used to change individual personality or to teach learners how to be self-motivated (Keller, 1987a).

Gagné's nine events of instruction and Keller's ARCS model

The four ARCS factors have an intertwined and interacting relationship, rather than a linear relationship. They can be implemented within Gagné's nine events of instruction. For example, as shown in Table 11, an instructor of a Web design class can incorporate ARCS strategies while delivering instruction based on the nine events of instruction.

Table 11. Designing Nine Events of Instruction with ARCS Strategies

Gagné's Events of Instruction	Keller's ARCS Strategies	Simplified Lesson Plan
1. Gain attention	• Attention-gaining strategies • Relevance-producing strategies	Show a completed Web survey form to students and explain "This is what you'll produce in this class today. You will earn 10 points for successfully creating a survey form at the end of the class."
2. Inform learners of objective	• Attention-gaining strategies • Relevance-producing strategies	List new Web design skills that students will learn in order to design a form page (e.g., set up a form, insert radio buttons and text boxes).

(continued)

Table 11. Designing Nine Events of Instruction with ARCS Strategies *(concluded)*

Gagné's Events of Instruction	Keller's ARCS Strategies	Simplified Lesson Plan
3. Stimulate recall of prior knowledge	• Relevance-producing strategies • Confidence-building strategies	Remind them of Web design skills that they learned previously (e.g., change font, insert bullet points). Tell them that they will use the skills again. Provide a job aid that outlines the overall steps of previously learned tasks.
4. Present new content	• Attention-gaining strategies • Relevance-producing strategies • Confidence-building strategies	Show several examples of Web-based forms used for surveys. Slowly show the steps for creating a form on the screen.
5. Provide learning guidance	• Confidence-building strategies	Provide a job aid. Explain several important steps to pay attention to.
6. Elicit performance	• Confidence-building strategies	Have students follow the steps in the job aid to create a form.
7. Provide feedback	• Confidence-building strategies • Satisfaction-generating strategies	Have them submit the form and see the results. Provide immediate feedback if the form does not function correctly.
8. Assess performance	• Confidence-building strategies • Satisfaction-generating strategies	Have students develop another form without help. Provide feedback after they finish the form.
9. Enhance retention and transfer	• Relevance-producing strategies • Confidence-building strategies • Satisfaction-generating strategies	Provide a homework assignment to create a survey form page of their choice. Have them show their products to classmates in a subsequent class.

References

Berg, S. A. (2007). *Gagné's nine events of instruction: A sample lesson plan.* Unpublished manuscript, Boise State University.

Briggs, L. J. (1970). *Handbook of procedures for the design of instruction* (Monograph No. 4). Washington, D.C.: American Institutes for Research.

Briggs, L. J., & Wagner, W. W. (1981). *Handbook of procedures for the design of instruction* (2nd ed.). Englewood Cliffs, NJ: Educational Technology Publications.

Chyung, S. Y. (2001). Systematic and systemic approaches to reducing attrition rates in online higher education. *American Journal of Distance Education, 15*(3), 36–49.

Dick, W. (1997). A model for the systematic design of instruction. In R. Tennyson, F. Schott, N. Seel, & S. Dijkstra (Eds.), *Instructional design: International perspective* (Vol. 1, pp. 361–369). Mahwah, NJ: Lawrence Erlbaum.

Dick, W., & Carey, L. (1978). *The systematic design of instruction* (1st ed.). New York: HarperCollins Publishers Inc.

Dick, W., & Carey, L. (1996). *The systematic design of instruction* (4th ed.). New York: HarperCollins Publishers Inc.

Dick, W., Carey, L., & Carey, J. (2005). *The systematic design of instruction* (6th ed.). Boston: Allyn & Bacon.

Gagné, R. M. (1962). Military training and principles of learning. *American Psychologist, 17,* 83–91.

Gagné, R. M. (1965). *The conditions of learning* (1st ed.). New York: Holt, Rinehart and Winston, Inc.

Gagné, R. M. (1970). *The conditions of learning* (2nd ed.). New York: Holt, Rinehart and Winston, Inc.

Gagné, R. M. (1977). *The conditions of learning* (3rd ed.). New York: Holt, Rinehart and Winston, Inc.

Gagné, R. M. (1985). *The conditions of learning* (4th ed.). New York: Holt, Rinehart and Winston, Inc.

Gagné, R. M. (1988). Mastery learning and instructional design. *Performance Improvement Quarterly, 1*(1), 7–18.

Gagné, R. M., & Medsker, K. (1996). *The conditions of learning: Training Applications.* Orlando, FL: Harcourt Brace College Publishers.

Gagné, R. M., & Rohwer Jr., W. D. (1969). Instructional psychology. *Annual Review of Psychology, 20,* 381–418.

Heinich, R., Molenda, M., & Russell, J. (1989). *Instructional media and the new technologies of instruction* (3rd ed.). New York: Macmillan Publishing Company.

Heinich, R., Molenda, M., Russell, J., & Smaldino, S. (1999). *Instructional media and technologies for learning* (6th ed.). Upper Saddle River, NJ: Prentice Hall.

Keller, J. (1987a). Development and use of the ARCS model of instructional design. *Journal of Instructional Development, 10*(3), 2–10.

Keller, J. (1987b). Strategies for stimulating the motivation to learn. *Performance and Instruction, 26*(8), 1–7.

Keller, J. (1987c). The systematic process of motivational design. *Performance and Instruction, 26*(9/10), 1–8.

Mager, R. F. (1962). *Preparing Instructional Objectives* (1st ed.). Palo Alto, CA: Fearon Publisher.

Mager, R. F. (1975). *Preparing Instructional Objectives* (2nd ed.). Belmont, CA: Fearon Publisher.

Mager, R. F. (1997). *Preparing Instructional Objectives* (3rd ed.). Atlanta, GA: The Center for Effective Performance, Inc.

Merriam-Webster's collegiate dictionary (11th ed.). (2003). Springfield, MA: Merriam-Webster.

Richey, R. C. (Ed.) (2000). *The legacy of Robert M. Gagné*. Syracuse, NY: ERIC Clearinghouse on Information and Technology.

Rosenberg, M. (1982, September). The ABCs of ISD. *Training & Development, 36*, 44–50.

Tennyson, R. D., & Schott, F. (1997). Instructional design theory, research, and models. In R. Tennyson, F. Schott, N. Seel, & S. Dijkstra (Eds.), *Instructional design: International perspective* (Vol. 1, pp. 1–16). Mahwah, NJ: Lawrence Erlbaum.

Evaluation of Training Programs

Systematic and Systemic Evaluation of Training Programs

Measure vs. evaluate	**mea·sure** \\'me-zhər, 'mā-\ *vt*

mea·sure \\'me-zhər, 'mā-\ *vt*
- to choose or control with cautious restraint
- to ascertain the measurements of
- to estimate or appraise by a criterion

(Merriam-Webster's Collegiate Dictionary, 2003, p. 769)

eval·u·ate \i-'val-yə-ˌwāt, -yü-ˌāt\ *vt*
- to determine or fix the value of
- to determine the significance, worth, or condition of usually by careful appraisal and study

(Merriam-Webster's Collegiate Dictionary, 2003, p. 432)

Evaluation

Evaluation is considered a form of applied research, but there is a slight difference between applied research and evaluation:

- *Applied research* is aimed at producing generalizable knowledge relevant to providing a solution to a general problem.

- *Evaluation* focuses on collecting specific information relevant to a particular or specific evaluation object or "evaluand" (Guba & Lincoln, 1981, cited in Worthen, Sanders, & Fitzpatrick, 1997). Specifically,

    — Evaluation is disciplined inquiry to make a judgment about the worth of the evaluation objects (such as instructional programs).
    — Evaluation produces information that is used to make decisions.

One example of evaluation: a study about the effectiveness of a new safety training program on reducing work-related injuries in an organization. If the results reveal that the work-related injury rate has been reduced by 12 percent after the training program is implemented, the organization might recognize the worth of the training program and decide to continue to provide it to the employees annually. The organization would still need to consider that other factors might have influenced the results.

Evaluation is conducted through various measurement processes, using quantitative methods, qualitative methods, or a combination of both.

Systematic and systemic evaluation

This chapter introduces Donald Kirkpatrick's four-level model of evaluation, which will help practitioners understand the systematic and systemic approaches to evaluating the effectiveness of training programs. This chapter also provides an overview of the main concepts in measurement and evaluation, and describes methods of constructing evaluation instruments.

Donald Kirkpatrick's Four-Level Model of Evaluation

Four levels
of evaluating
training programs

About a half century ago, Donald Kirkpatrick, now professor emeritus at the University of Wisconsin, was working on his Ph.D. at the University of Wisconsin. He decided that his doctoral dissertation would focus on evaluating a supervisory training program. He came up with the idea of "measuring participants' reaction to the program, the amount of learning that took place, the extent of their change in behavior after they returned to their jobs, and any final results that were achieved by participants after they returned to work" (Kirkpatrick, 1996b, p. 55). The practice of using four levels in evaluating training programs came out of his work. The levels are (1) reaction, (2) learning, (3) behavior, and (4) results. Although he originally called them "steps" in the article published in the November 1959 issue of *Training and Development*, "levels" is more widely used to refer to his evaluation model (Kirkpatrick, 1996b).

Kirkpatrick (1978, 1996a) explains that there are three reasons for evaluating training programs and that his evaluation model is useful for any of the three reasons:

1. To know how to improve future programs
2. To determine whether to continue or discontinue the program
3. To justify the existence of the training program or department

Each level of Kirkpatrick's evaluation model requires one to elicit different information on the effectiveness of a training program:

1. Reaction: Did the participants like the training program?
2. Learning outcomes: Did they learn what they were supposed to learn? How much did they learn?
3. Behavioral change: Did they change their on-the-job behavior?
4. Results on the organization: Did their knowledge and changed behavior positively affect the organization in terms of resulting in increased production, improved quality, decreased costs, etc.? (Kirkpatrick & Kirkpatrick, 2005a, 2005b)

Kirkpatrick's four-level model of evaluation helps practitioners measure the effectiveness of a training program from level 1 to level 4 in a *systematic* way, but also encourages them to project its *systemic* impact on long-term outcomes as well as short-term outcomes.

Kirkpatrick (1996a) explains that "trainers must begin with desired results and then determine what behavior is needed to accomplish them. . . . The four levels of evaluation are considered in reverse. First, we evaluate reaction. Then we evaluate learning, behavior, and results" (p. 26). In other words, the four levels of evaluation should be strategically aligned with the levels of goals, as shown with numbering in Table 12 (see also Phillips, 2002).

Table 12. The Relationship between Goal Setting and Evaluation

Goals and Objectives	Evaluations
1. Organizational goals ↓	8. Results ↑
2. Performance objectives ↓	7. Behavior ↑
3. Instructional objectives ↓	6. Learning ↑
4. Motivational objectives	5. Reaction ↑

Note: Although the terms *performance objectives* and *instructional objectives* are used synonymously in some of the literature (e.g., Dick, Carey, & Carey, 2005), in this case, a performance objective refers to an objective that focuses on behavioral changes *on the job* after completing instruction, whereas an instructional objective refers to a learning outcome to be accomplished *within a given instruc tional context.*

Here is a hypothetical scenario:

A large consulting firm decided to upgrade its old training system to a new knowledge management system to make its business process more efficient and effective. With the new system, the company would be able to provide just-in-time information to clients and employees, which will increase the company's annual revenue by 12 percent. An analysis after launching the new system revealed that most employees were not using the system because they did not know how to use it and they would need to receive training. When they return to their work environment after training, they would be required to share various data and information via the new system. Training hasn't even started, but a lot of employees are expressing negative attitudes toward this mandated change, which seem to be having a negative impact on their attitudes toward attending the training.

One strategic approach to dealing with a situation like the one above would be to clearly state the organizational goals, performance objectives, instructional objectives, and motivational objectives, and to conduct four-level evaluations. Table 13 illustrates how this is done.

Table 13. A Strategic Approach to Designing Goals and Evaluations

Goal	Evaluation
1. Organizational goal: The consulting firm will increase its annual revenue by 12%.	8. Evaluation on results: Has the 12% annual revenue been achieved? Million ($) — **Revenue by Quarter** 150 125 100 1st qtr 2nd qtr 3rd qtr 4th qtr
2. Performance objective: After they return to their job, the employees should be able to use the new knowledge management system (KMS) without help.	7. Evaluation on behavior: Are they using the new KMS? Freq (#) — **Behavioral Change** 10 8 .... 8 6 4 2 — 3 0 Before training After training

3. Instructional objective: At the end of instruction, the trainees should be able to do the following correctly:
 	
  a. Log in to the KMS
  b. Retrieve data from the KMS
  c. Upload data to the KMS
  d. Recognize the structure of information flow via the KMS
  e. Explain the benefits of using the KMS
	6. Evaluation on learning: Did they learn?
	
	% — **Test Score** — 96
	100
	80 62
	60
	40
	20
	0
	Pretest Posttest

4. Motivational objective: During the instruction, the trainees will be motivated to learn the features of the new KMS that enable them to increase the efficiency and effectiveness of business processes.	5. Evaluation on reaction: Was the training motivationally appealing? % — **Satisfaction** 100 80 68 60 40 20 9 23 0 Disagree Neutral Agree

Constructing "Smile" Sheets

Reaction sheets or "smile" sheets

The level 1 evaluation is conducted at the end of instruction to measure participants' immediate reactions to the program using a survey questionnaire. For that reason, it is referred to as a *reaction sheet*. Because its purpose is to measure the participants' satisfaction levels, it is sometimes referred to as a *smile sheet*.

Level 1 evaluation questionnaires measure participants' *attitudinal status* toward the program. The Likert scale (strongly agree, agree, undecided, disagree, and strongly disagree) is often used as a response mode for statements that measure *attitudinal status*. It was developed by a social psychologist named Rensis Likert in 1932 as part of his doctoral dissertation at Columbia University.

Suggestions for writing attitude statements

Kubiszyn and Borich (1996) provide the following suggestions for writing statements that measure attitudinal status:

1. Write simple, clear, and direct sentences.
2. Write short statements.
3. Avoid negatives, especially double negatives.
4. Avoid factual statements.
5. Avoid reference to the past.
6. Avoid absolutes such as *all, none, always,* and *never*.
7. Avoid nondistinguishing statements.
8. Avoid irrelevancies.
9. Use *only, merely,* and *just* sparingly.
10. Use one thought per statement. (pp. 207–208)

These are helpful guidelines for constructing statements in level 1 evaluation questionnaires. Table 14 shows *why* and *how* the initial statements should be revised. (Note: The Likert scale is used in the examples.)

Table 14. Examples of Questionnaire Statements to be Revised

Before Revision	Reasons for Revision	After Revision
This new training was no better than the previous one.	Write a clear and direct sentence. Avoid reference to the past.	The training was presented in an interesting manner.
The objectives were not clearly stated.	Avoid negatives.	The objectives were clearly stated.
The content was relevant to my job and the instructor helped me build confidence.	Use one thought per statement. (Write two statements.)	1. The content was relevant to my job. 2. The instructor helped me build confidence.

Evaluating reaction based on the ARCS factors

The purpose of using the ARCS model is to improve the motivational appeal of instruction—in other words, to improve the participants' reaction to the instruction. Therefore, the ARCS model can be used as a framework for constructing pre-assessment (to develop motivational objectives) or evaluation questionnaires (to measure the outcomes), as described below:

- Use the ARCS model as a framework to develop a pre-assessment questionnaire in order to determine whether or not the instruction should be revised to improve its motivational appeal.

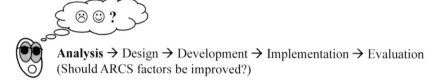

Analysis → Design → Development → Implementation → Evaluation
(Should ARCS factors be improved?)

- Use the ARCS model as a framework to develop a level 1 evaluation questionnaire after it has been used to improve the motivational appeal of the instruction in order to find out whether or not the revised instruction was indeed effective in improving its motivational appeal.

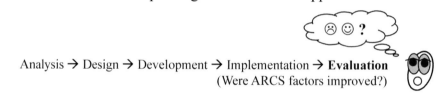

Analysis → Design → Development → Implementation → **Evaluation**
(Were ARCS factors improved?)

For example, suppose that existing instruction has been revised with new learning activities, examples, and exercises to improve its motivational appeal in all four ARCS areas. The examples in Table 15 intend to measure the effectiveness of specific ARCS factors addressed in this case.

Table 15. Examples of Evaluation Questions to Measure ARCS Factors

Evaluation	ARCS
The learning activities helped me focus on important parts of the instruction. Strongly disagree 1 2 3 4 5 Strongly agree	Attention
The examples used in instruction were relevant to my job. Strongly disagree 1 2 3 4 5 Strongly agree	Relevance
The exercises were appropriately challenging. Strongly disagree 1 2 3 4 5 Strongly agree	Confidence
I feel satisfied with the amount of knowledge that I gained from the instruction. Strongly disagree 1 2 3 4 5 Strongly agree	Satisfaction

Measurement Scales

Four types of measurement scales

One of the first steps in constructing evaluation instruments is to determine *what to measure* and *how to measure it*. Stanley Smith Stevens, a professor of psychology at Harvard University, explains this: "in the broadest sense, [measurement] is defined as the assignment of numerals to objects or events according to rules. The fact that numerals can be assigned under different rules leads to different kinds of scales and different kinds of measurements" (Stevens, 1946, p. 677). He classified four types of measurement scales:

1. A nominal scale

A nominal scale labels something with a name, and no rank-orders are assumed among different labels. Nominal measurement is "a process of grouping objects into classes so that all of those in a single class are equivalent (or nearly so) with respect to some attribute or property" (Glass & Stanley, 1970, p. 8). For example:

- Gender: male or female
- Nationality: American, Chinese, French, German, Korean, etc.
- Job satisfaction factors: motivating factors and hygiene factors
- Leadership styles: autocratic, transactional, participative, or transformational

2. An ordinal scale

An ordinal scale is used during the operation of rank-ordering (Stevens, 1946). Here are a few examples:

- Preferred locations for retirement: 1. Boise, Idaho; 2. Denver, Colorado; 3. Tucson, Arizona
- Military ranks: Lieutenant, Captain, Major, Colonel, General

3. An interval scale

In an interval scale, there is an equal distance between the intervals, but there is no absolute zero value, though often an arbitrary zero value is assigned. Here are some examples:

- Days in a calendar: The difference between March 1 and March 5 and the difference between April 6 and April 10 are the same, but no absolute-zero day exists in a calendar.
- Celsius temperature scales: The difference between 35 and 40 and the difference between 40 and 45 in Celsius are the same, but zero degrees in Celsius does not mean "no temperature."

The Likert scale (Strongly disagree, Disagree, Undecided, Agree, Strongly agree) can be viewed as an ordinal scale, but it is now common to accept it as an interval scale by treating the distances between the intervals to be approximately the same (e.g., Tuckman, 1994).

4. A ratio scale

In a ratio scale, there is an equal distance between intervals, and it has an absolute zero value, which indicates the absence of the attribute measured. Here are some examples:

- Length
- Weight
- Height
- Time

The relationship among scales

In the order provided above (nominal, ordinal, interval, and ratio), each successive measurement scale possesses its unique characteristics as well as the characteristics of each lower scale (see Table 16):

- An ordinal scale uses labels or names (a characteristic of a nominal scale) to rank-order them according to its selected rule.
- An interval scale also tells the order of items (a characteristic of an ordinal scale), while it also shows the same distance between the items.
- A ratio scale labels the measured units, tells the rank-order, claims an equal distance between the intervals, and has an absolute zero point.

Table 16. A Comparison of the Characteristics of Four Scales

Nominal	Ordinal	Interval	Ratio
Named based on similar property	• Named based on similar property • Ordered based on the degrees of the property	• Named based on similar property • Ordered based on the degrees of the property • Having equal differences between intervals	• Named based on similar property • Ordered based on the degrees of the property • Having equal differences between intervals • Having an absolute zero point

Response Modes

Various
response modes

Constructing an evaluation questionnaire requires a decision on how each question should be stated and answered (i.e., selection of response modes). There are various types of response modes. An appropriate response mode should be selected based on the purpose of asking the question and the type of data to be obtained. Here are several examples:

1. Likert scale

The learning management system is user-friendly.

Strongly disagree ___ Disagree ___ Undecided ___ Agree ___ Strongly agree ___

(Note: "Uncertain" or "Neutral" can be substituted for "Undecided.")

2. Likert-like scaled response

The instructor was _____ available when I needed help.

always ___   often ___   seldom ___   never ___

3. Opposing-polarities adjective scale

The PowerPoint presentation was

interesting   1   2   3   4   5   6   7   boring

4. Ranking response

Rank the effectiveness of the following media used during instruction:

___ PowerPoint presentations   ___ computer-based practices   ___ videotapes

5. Checklist response

How many times a week do you use this manual?

___ 0   ___ 1–10   ___ 11 or more

6. Categorical response

Would you recommend this program to your coworkers?

Yes ___   No ___

7. Fill-in-blank

How long have you been working for this company?

___ years ___ months

Conducting Four-Level Evaluations: An Example

Kirkpatrick's
four-level model
of evaluation
in action
(Stebner, 2007)

What follows is a scenario where Kirkpatrick's four-level model of evaluation was applied to measure the effectiveness of training on four levels of outcomes.

Monetary losses due to fraudulent new accounts have increased in the last six months at a major bank in the United States. To solve the problem, programmers have modified certain fields within the opening-a-new-account program to require predefined criteria. However, it became apparent that many new account representatives were not following mandatory compliance guidelines for the company's Know Your Customer program and the U.S. Patriot Act, because they were not familiar with the information.

The solution requested by executive management is to provide a half-day program to train new account reps on these field modifications and to also review new account compliance, including Know Your Customer guidelines and the U.S. Patriot Act. The training will be conducted in classrooms that have computers tied to a training database so that the trainees can practice the new procedures without affecting real customers.

To measure the effectiveness of the training program, four-level evaluations will be conducted, as planned below.

Level 1. Reaction

At the end of the training, an evaluation form will be distributed to each participant and collected as participants exit the training room. The evaluation form consists of five statements measured on a Likert scale and three open-ended questions to determine the overall satisfaction of each participant with the course and the trainer (see Exhibit 1).

Level 2. Learning Outcomes

The level 2 evaluation will be conducted with two different components:

1. One week prior to the training, participants will take a pretest consisting of multiple-choice questions that measure their understanding about the Know Your Customer program and the U.S. Patriot Act. At the end of the training, the same test will be administered to compare the scores.

2. Participants will be presented with three different new-account scenarios that deal with a compliance issue or a fraudulent account "red flag." They will be asked to propose appropriate actions. The trainer will review the responses, score them, and provide feedback to the participants.

Level 3. Behavioral Change

Two weeks after training, the Fraud/Security department will run a report on each participant that lists any accounts opened that were flagged as either suspicious or fraudulent accounts. Those employees with one or more flags will be interviewed to analyze the causes. If they still lack knowledge, they will receive additional coaching and/or be asked to take the class again. *Note* that Level 3 evaluation begins as early as two weeks after the training, due to the severity of the issue.

Level 4. Results

Each month after training, the Fraud/Security department will compare fraud losses with losses incurred prior to the inception of training.

Exhibit 1. Example of a level 1 evaluation form.

Evaluation Form

Instructor's name: _____ Program title: _____

This is an anonymous evaluation. Your feedback will help us evaluate this program and improve the quality of the program. Thanks.

1. The stated objectives were met.
   Strongly disagree ___ Disagree ___ Undecided ___ Agree ___ Strongly agree ___

2. The class length was the right amount of time.
   Strongly disagree ___ Disagree ___ Undecided ___ Agree ___ Strongly agree ___

3. The trainer was knowledgeable.
   Strongly disagree ___ Disagree ___ Undecided ___ Agree ___ Strongly agree ___

4. I will be able to apply this information.
   Strongly disagree ___ Disagree ___ Undecided ___ Agree ___ Strongly agree ___

5. The reference materials will be useful to me back on the job.
   Strongly disagree ___ Disagree ___ Undecided ___ Agree ___ Strongly agree ___

6. What was the most valuable part of this training?

7. What was the least valuable part of this training?

8. What suggestions do you have to improve this training?

Level 1
evaluation report

After the level 1 evaluation is administered, the data need to be analyzed. To score the data obtained from a Likert scale, numbers 1 through 5 are assigned to the five points of the scale (Likert, Roslow, & Murphy, 1993). There are two ways to do so, as shown below:

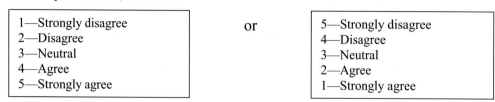

1—Strongly disagree
2—Disagree
3—Neutral
4—Agree
5—Strongly agree

or

5—Strongly disagree
4—Disagree
3—Neutral
2—Agree
1—Strongly agree

For example, suppose that 50 responses were obtained from statement #1:

1. The stated objectives were met.

   Strongly disagree ___   Disagree ___   Undecided ___   Agree ___   Strongly agree ___

If the coding scheme in the left column shown above is used, the average score of the data obtained from statement #1 would be calculated in the following manner:

Table 17. A Method for Calculating Results

	Strongly disagree	**Disagree**	**Neutral**	**Agree**	**Strongly agree**
C: Codification	1	2	3	4	5
R: # of responses	6	5	1	17	21
C multiplied by R	6	10	3	68	105

The total score is 192 (6 + 10 + 3 + 68 + 105). Therefore, the average score is 3.84 (192 ÷ 50) on a scale of 1 to 5 when 1 is strongly disagree and 5 is strongly agree. In this case, the higher the average score, the better.

However, the average score itself does not provide information about the 11 respondents who selected "Disagree" or "Strongly disagree." Therefore, it is useful to provide the frequency in a table or a bar graph such as the one in Figure 12.

1. The stated objectives were met.

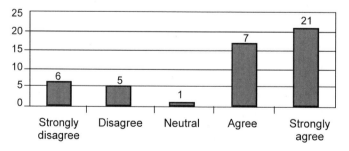

Figure 12. A bar graph showing level 1 results.

References

Dick, W., L. Carey, & Carey, J. (2005). *The systematic design of instruction* (6th ed.). Boston: Allyn and Bacon.

Glass, G., & Stanley, J. (1970). *Statistical methods in education and psychology.* Englewood Cliffs, NJ: Prentice-Hall.

Kirkpatrick, D. L. (1978, September). Evaluating in-house training programs. *Training & Development Journal, 32,* 6–9.

Kirkpatrick, D. L. (1996a). *Evaluating training programs: The four levels* (1st ed.). San Francisco: Berrett-Koehler Publishers.

Kirkpatrick, D. L. (1996b, January). Great ideas revisited. *Training & Development Journal, 50,* 54–59.

Kirkpatrick, D. L., & Kirkpatrick, J. D. (2005a). *Evaluating training programs: The four levels* (3rd ed.). San Francisco: Berrett-Koehler Publishers.

Kirkpatrick, D. L., & Kirkpatrick, J. D. (2005b). *Transferring learning to behavior: Using the four levels to improve performance.* San Francisco: Berrett-Koehler Publishers, Inc.

Kubiszyn, T., & Borich, G. (1996). *Educational testing and measurement* (5th ed.). New York: HarperCollins College Publishers.

Likert, R. (1932). A technique for the measurement of attitudes. *Archives of Psychology, 140,* 5–55.

Likert, R., Roslow, S., & Murphy, G. (1993). A simple and reliable method for scoring the Thurstone attitude scales. *Personnel Psychology, 46*(3), 689–690.

Merriam-Webster's collegiate dictionary (11th ed.). (2003). Springfield, MA: Merriam-Webster.

Phillips, J. (2003). *Measuring the return on investment in training and development.* Conference handouts distributed at the ASTD Treasure Valley Conference, Boise, Idaho.

Phillips, P. (2002). *The bottomline on ROI.* Atlanta, GA: CEP Press.

Stebner, M. (2007). *Conducting systematic evaluations with Kirkpatrick's 4 level model of evaluation.* Unpublished manuscript, Boise State University.

Stevens, S. S. (1946). On the theory of scales of measurement. *Science, 103,* 677–680.

Tuckman, B. (1994). *Conducting educational research* (4th ed.). Orlando, FL: Harcourt Brace College Publishers.

Worthen, B. R., Sanders, J. R., & Fitzpatrick, J. L. (1997). *Program evaluation: Alternative approaches and practical guidelines* (2nd ed.). White Plains, NY: Longman Publishers.

Chapter

5

Systems Approaches to Instructional Development

Instructional Systems Development

Systems
approaches to
instructional
development

Bela Banathy, an educator and researcher, devoted his career to studying educational systems. As he explains in his 1968 work, the terms *systems concept* and *systems approach* emerged during and after World War II. The research and development activities for developing complex man-machine systems at that time revealed that one could not simply add new components to an existing system such as an aircraft and expect it to function properly. He explains his views this way:

> What emerged from this realization was a new method of planning and development in which designers learned that they first had to identify the purpose and performance expectations of the system before they could develop all the parts that made up the system as a whole. It is the system as a whole—and not its parts separately—that must be planned, designed, developed, installed, and managed. What is really significant is not how the individual components function separately, but the way they interact and are integrated into the system for the purpose of achieving the goal of the system. Generalizing from this example, *systems* can be defined as *deliberately designed synthetic organisms, comprised of interrelated and interacting components which are employed to function in an integrated fashion to attain predetermined purposes.* (p. 2)

Systems approach is then defined as "the application of the systems view, or systems thinking, to human endeavors" such as instructional development (p. 13).

In the history of the development of the instructional design field, the decade of the 1970s is often characterized as "the decade of the systems approach" (Dick, 1987, p. 189). Andrews and Goodson (1980, 1995) found that as many as 40 systematic instructional design models with *a systems approach* to various degrees were published in the late 1960s and the 1970s (e.g., Briggs, 1970; Kaufman, 1972). Only four of them were published in the 1960s. One of the models this era produced was the *Interservice Instructional Systems Development Model*, developed by Branson and others in 1976 (Branson & Grow, 1987). This model consists of five structured phases: analyze, design, develop, implement, and control. This resembles what is now known as the ADDIE processes (analyze, design, develop, implement, and evaluate).

ADDIE with
training needs
assessment

This chapter provides an overview of the ADDIE model as the primary structure of instructional systems development processes. It also explains the meaning of the term *training needs assessment* from a historical perspective to point out the paradigm shift from training focus to performance focus.

The ADDIE Model

Linear or
non-linear

ADDIE is the term used to describe a systematic approach to instructional development. The acronym refers to the five major phases included in the generic instructional systems development (ISD) process: analysis, design, development, implementation, and evaluation. The identity of the individual who came up with the acronym in the first place is unclear, but the ADDIE-like approach was used by practitioners during the 1970s. The actual acronym started appearing in literature in the 1980s.

A variety of illustrations have been proposed to represent the ADDIE model. It can be illustrated as a systematic, *linear* procedure, as shown in Figure 13 (e.g., Rossett, 1987). In this illustration, each phase is followed step-by-step, while the data obtained from the analysis phase are fed back to each of the subsequent steps:

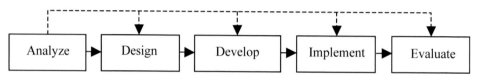

Figure 13. Linear ADDIE steps.

The ADDIE steps can also be illustrated as a linear but cyclical procedure, as shown in Figure 14 (e.g., Piskurich & Sanders, 1998):

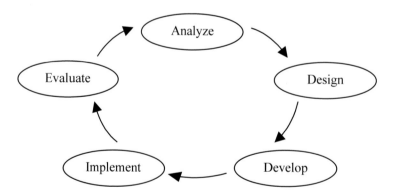

Figure 14. Linear, cyclical ADDIE steps.

Perhaps a more useful illustration of the ADDIE model is to present it as an interrelated, systemic, *non-linear* procedure, where each one of the first four phases is interacting with the "evaluation" phase to validate its outputs, which will become inputs of the next phase, as shown in Figure 15 (e.g., Molenda, 2003; Rosenberg, 1982; The U.S. Coast Guard, 1984).

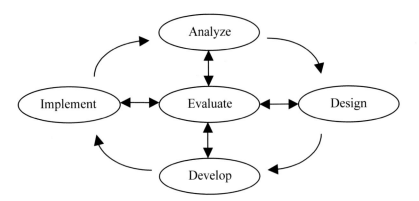

Figure 15. Non-linear ADDIE steps.

In other words, each of the analysis, design, development, and implementation phases of the ADDIE model includes an *evaluation* component. For example, Rosenberg (1982) explains that:

• Evaluation during the *analysis* phase is necessary to determine how well the needs of organization, learners, and the job were researched and analyzed, since the information would be used as inputs for designing appropriate instructional materials.

• Evaluation during the *design* phase is done to ensure that instructional objectives support the job performance requirements and that instructional strategies as well as the test instruments are appropriately selected to facilitate the achievement of the instructional objectives.

• Evaluation during the *development* phase is to examine whether or not the instructional materials, media, and the test instruments are complete and valid according to the design specifications.

• Evaluation during the *implementation* phase is conducted to determine the readiness of the instructional system, including the instructor, facilities, and instructional materials. Potential changes in the instructional system are assessed, since the implementation phase usually requires that there be an ongoing process of monitoring and adapting as changes are made over time.

Putting ADDIE into practice

The ADDIE model provides an overall structure of *systematic* and *systemic* approaches to instructional development. However, it does not provide information about exactly what should be done during each step. It is the practitioner's responsibility to select and complete appropriate tasks in each step. Table 18 presents sample tasks to be performed in each phase of the ADDIE model, as well as examples of useful theories, concepts, and models to be used to complete such tasks.

Table 18. Sample Tasks and Theories to be Used in the
ADDIE Phases of Instructional Development

ADDIE Phase	Sample Tasks to be Performed	Examples of Useful Theories, Concepts, and Models
Analyze	• Conduct a training needs assessment • Conduct a learner analysis • Conduct a job/task analysis	• Rossett's training needs assessment (Rossettt, 1987) • Keller's ARCS model for assessing learner motivation (Keller, 1987) • Bloom's taxonomy of educational objectives (Bloom et al., 1956) • Gagné's five domains of learning (Gagné, 1985)
Design	• Write instructional objectives • Design test instruments • Design instructional strategies • Design a lesson plan • Identify instructional resources	• Mager's method of preparing instructional objectives (Mager, 1997) • Bloom's taxonomy for ensuring congruence (Bloom et al., 1956) • Thorndike's laws (Thorndike, 1912) • Gagné's nine events of instruction (Gagné, 1985) • Keller's ARCS model for developing motivational strategies (Keller, 1987)
Develop	• Develop instructor guide, student guide, workbooks, and job aids • Develop instructional materials and media	• The ASSURE model (Heinich, Molenda, Russell, & Smaldino, 1999) • The use of job aids (Harless, 1986; Rossett & Gautier-Downes, 1991)
Implement and Evaluate	• Deliver instruction • Facilitate implementation processes • Conduct formative evaluation and make changes if necessary • Conduct summative evaluation	• Keller's ARCS model for developing evaluation instruments (Keller, 1987) • Tyler's idea of conducting repeated evaluations to improve quality (Tyler, 1949) • Kirkpatrick's four-level model of evaluation (Kirkpatrick, 1996) • Return on investment (Phillips, 2003)

Training Needs Assessment

Training needs assessment

Allison Rossett, a professor at San Diego State University, published *Training Needs Assessment* in 1987 in which she explained that "Training needs assessment (TNA) is an umbrella term for the analysis activities trainers use to examine and understand performance problems or new technologies" (p. 14). Rossett (1987) explains that during a training needs assessment, trainers seek information about the following:

- **Optimal** performance or knowledge
- **Actual** or current performance or knowledge
- **Feelings** of trainees and others
- **Causes** of the problem from many perspectives
- **Solutions** to the problem from many perspectives (p. 4)

Various methods of collecting data can be used during a training needs assessment, such as interviews, observations, focus groups, surveys, and extant data analysis.

Rossett (1987, 1995) explains that there are three types of situations that call for a (training) needs assessment:

1. Introduction of new initiatives
2. Mandated training
3. Performance problems

For example, the situation below would fall into the *new initiatives* category that calls for a training needs assessment:

> The Office Technology Committee of a law firm consisting of 270 attorneys and staff decided to replace their old intranet software with Microsoft Sharepoint as the new intranet portal service for the firm. This is in line with the firm's Information Technology strategy. . . . It was decided that approximately 25 staff members would become Editors of the Web pages on the new intranet. Each person is required to attend training classes (Basics, Intermediate, and Advanced) in hopes that they would become exemplary performers. (Anderson, 2006, p. 12)

Rossett (1995) explains that the purpose of conducting a training needs assessment caused by a new initiative is to determine the optimal level of performance and the feelings about the change. Therefore, the training needs assessment in the above situation is intended to reveal information about the optimal level of the intranet editors' performance and their feelings about the job, confidence levels, preferred topics for training, etc.

Two examples of *mandated training* are annual safety training and sexual harassment prevention training. The lack of knowledge or skills may or may not be the reason why these types of mandated training programs are being provided. Therefore, Rossett (1995) suggests treating them as either a new initiative or a performance problem.

Rossett (1995) explains that a *performance problem*, such as a fast food restaurant experiencing a downfall of its revenue, also calls for a training needs assessment. The purpose is to identify the optimal performance level, the actual performance level, and the causes of the performance problem. However, other authors have questioned whether or not the term *training needs assessment* implies that training is assumed as a solution. They suggest that the term *training requirements analysis* be used instead to reduce confusion (Watkins & Kaufman, 1996).

Training needs assessment vs. performance analysis

About a decade after she published *Training Needs Assessment*, Rossett published *First Things Fast* (1999), in which she describes performance analysis in detail. She explains the difference between *performance analysis* and *training needs assessment* this way:

> Performance analysis is what you do first and fast. Training needs assessment is what you do to create the tangible solution(s) to the problem or opportunity. Whereas performance analysis is the first response, needs assessment is the more measured and production-oriented effort. . . . Performance analysis helps you determine what to recommend. If training or information or references are indicated, then training needs assessment enables that recommendation to become a focused program. (pp. 24–25)

In other words, during performance analysis, it is not assumed that training is a solution. Training needs assessment is conducted only if the performance analysis has revealed that training is a solution to the performance problem (see Figure 16).

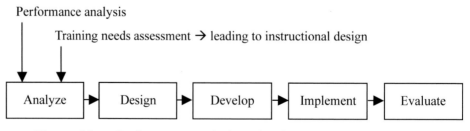

Figure 16.   Performance analysis and training needs assessment during the analysis phase of the ADDIE processes.

When to train vs. when not to train

In a way, the term *training needs assessment* reflects the shift in the practitioners' mindset from training focus to performance focus. As practitioners realized that instruction could not be an effective solution to *all* performance problems, they started putting more emphasis on conducting a comprehensive assessment up front, even if training was initially requested. Other terms such as *performance analysis* and *front-end analysis* offer a broader and clearer meaning for their effort to carefully analyze the nature of the performance problem and to determine an appropriate type of solutions, whether it is an instructional type or a noninstructional type.

Figure 17 illustrates this changed mindset among leading practitioners and a new approach to handling performance issues. When a performance analysis concludes that instruction is necessary, practitioners continue with the remaining ADDIE steps by using various instructional methods and strategies, such as the ones described in the previous chapters of this book. When noninstructional interventions are called for, the same ADDIE steps, but with a different focus, could be followed. This holistic view for dealing with performance problems helps practitioners keep in mind the question of "when to train and when not to train" before deciding "how to train."

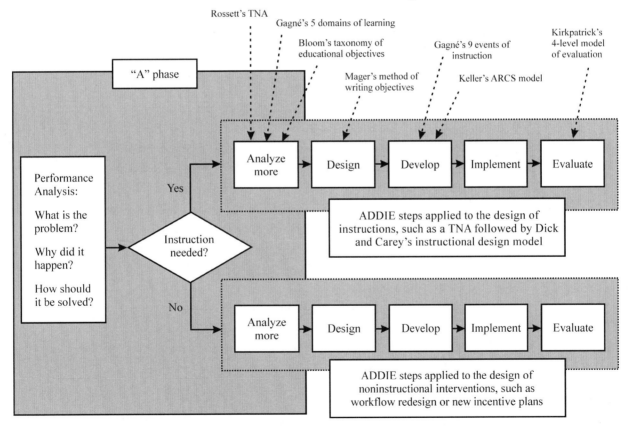

Figure 17. Application of ADDIE steps to the design of instruction and the design of noninstructional interventions that depend on the conclusion of a performance analysis.

References

Anderson, P. (2006). *IPT toolkit.* Unpublished manuscript, Boise State University.

Andrews, D. H., & Goodson, L. A. (1980). A comparative analysis of models of instructional design. *Journal of Instructional Development, 3*(4), 2–16.

Andrews, D. H., & Goodson, L. A. (1995). A comparative analysis of models of instructional design. In G. Anglin (Ed.), *Instructional technology: Past, present, and future* (2ⁿᵈ ed., pp. 161–182). Englewood, CO: Libraries Unlimited.

Banathy, B. H. (1968). *Instructional systems.* Palo Alto, CA: Fearon Publishers.

Bloom, B. S., Engelhart, M. D., Furst, E. J., Hill, W. H., & Krathwohl, D. R. (1956). *Taxonomy of educational objectives: The classification of educational goals (Handbook I: Cognitive domain).* New York: David McKay Company, Inc.

Branson, R. K., & Grow, G. (1987). Instructional systems development. In R. M. Gagné (Ed.), *Instructional technology: Foundations* (pp. 397–428). Hillsdale, NJ: Lawrence Erlbaum Associates.

Briggs, L. J., (1970). *Handbook of procedures for the design of instruction* (Monograph No. 4). Washington, D.C.: American Institutes for Research.

Dick, W. (1987). A history of instructional design and its impact on educational psychology. In J. A. Glover, & R. R. Ronning (Eds.). *Historical foundations of educational psychology* (pp. 183–202). New York: Plenum Press.

Gagné, R. M. (1985). *The conditions of learning* (4ᵗʰ ed.). New York: Holt, Rinehart and Winston, Inc.

Harless, J. (1986). Guiding performance with job aids. In D. Brethower (Ed.), *Introduction to performance technology* (Vol. 1, pp. 106–124). Washington, D.C.: The National Society for Performance and Instruction.

Heinich, R., Molenda, M., Russell, J., & Smaldino, S. (1999). *Instructional media and technologies for learning* (6ᵗʰ ed.). Upper Saddle River, NJ: Prentice Hall.

Kaufman, R. (1972). *Educational system planning.* Englewood Cliffs, NJ: Prentice-Hall.

Keller, J. (1987). Development and use of the ARCS model of instructional design. *Journal of Instructional Development, 10*(3), 2–10.

Kirkpatrick, D. L. (1996). *Evaluating training programs: The four levels.* San Francisco: Berrett-Koehler Publishers.

Mager, R. (1997). *Preparing instructional objectives* (3ʳᵈ ed.). Atlanta, GA: The Center for Effective Performance, Inc.

Molenda, M. (2003). In search of elusive ADDIE model. *Performance Improvement, 42*(5), 34–36.

Phillips, J. (2003). *Return on investment in training and performance improvement programs* (2ⁿᵈ ed.). Burlington, MA: Butterworth-Heinemann.

Piskurich, G. M., & Sanders, E. S. (1998). *ASTD models for learning technologies: Roles, competencies, and outputs.* Alexandria, VA: American Society for Training & Development.

Rosenberg, M. J. (1982, September). The ABCs of ISD. *Training & Development Journal, 36*, 44–50.

Rossett, A. (1987). *Training needs assessment.* Englewood Cliffs, NJ: Educational Technology Publications.

Rossett, A. (1995). Needs assessment. In G. Anglin (Ed.), *Instructional technology: Past, present, and future* (2nd ed., pp. 183–196). Englewood, CO: Libraries Unlimited.

Rossett, A. (1999). *First things fast: A handbook for performance analysis.* San Francisco: Jossey-Bass, Pfeiffer.

Rossett, A., & Gautier-Downes, J. (1991). *A handbook of job aids.* San Francisco, CA: Joessey-Bass.

The U. S. Coast Guard (1984). *Coast Guard training: A systems approach.* Unpublished manuscript by the U.S. Coast Guard, the U.S. Department of Transportation.

Thorndike, E. L. (1912). *Education, a first book.* New York: The Macmillan Company.

Tyler, R. W. (1949). *Basic principles of curriculum and instruction.* Chicago: The University of Chicago Press.

Watkins, R., & Kaufman, R. (1996). An update on relating needs assessment and needs analysis. *Performance Improvement, 35*(10), 10–13.

Human Performance Technology

Evolution of Human Performance Technology

Paradigm shift in instructional development

In the 19th century, Joseph Lancaster of England developed a monitorial method for teaching a large number of students. The Lancasterian type of instruction was practice-centered (Saettler, 1968), sometimes illustrated with a "mind as a muscle" metaphor (Baker, 1973 as cited in Shrock, 1995).

Since then, there have been several developmental phases of the instructional technology field that prompted people to think beyond this "muscle" metaphor. For example, as behaviorism became a dominant paradigm in educational psychology, the design of instruction was based on behavioral principles (or laws) of learning. The "mind as an itinerary" analogy illustrates the method used in programmed instruction, which is based on the principles of learning and teaching derived from behavioral psychology.

Beginning in the late 1960s, cognitivism started gaining in popularity. Cognitive psychologists and researchers focused on studying memory structure (a.k.a., schema). The "mind as a filing cabinet" analogy describes the influence of cognitive psychology on instructional development, as it focused on constructing meaningfully organized schema that would facilitate effective storage, retrieval, and use of memory (i.e., learning, remembering, and using).

Paradigm shift from behavior-focused to performance-focused

Human performance technology as a field of study evolved from the instructional technology field when practitioners began to see that instruction is not a cure-all. In many cases, other interventions have to be utilized, and the focus has to be on performance improvement. This was outside-the-box thinking.

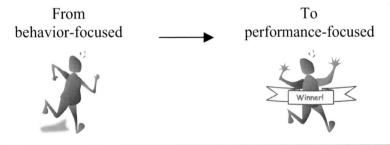

From
behavior-focused

To
performance-focused

Human performance technology as a field of study

This chapter explains the differences between learning and instruction, and behavioral change and performance. It then introduces human performance technology as a field of study and describes various performance improvement interventions.

Learning, Behavioral Change, and Performance

Learning vs. instruction

Instruction and *learning* are not the same thing. Instruction, which is defined as "a set of events that affect learners in such a way that learning is facilitated" (Gagné, Briggs & Wager, 1992, p. 3), is intended to help people learn. But instruction is not the only means to learning. Learning can occur while reading a newspaper, listening to the radio, or watching somebody else's performance. In other words, people gain new knowledge not only from *formal instruction*, but also through *noninstructional methods*.

Learning vs. performance

per·for·mance \pə(r)-ˈfor-mən(t)s\ *n*
1: a: the execution of an action
   b: something accomplished: DEED, FEAT
2: the fulfillment of a claim, promise, or request: IMPLEMENTATION

(Merriam-Webster's Collegiate Dictionary, 2003, p. 920)

Learning and *performance* are not the same thing. Acquisition of new knowledge might not be enough or even necessary for a person to perform a new task or to raise his or her current performance level. New knowledge can help us exhibit a new behavior, and the new behavior is a means for improving performance.

That is, performance is about outcomes: "Behavior is individual activity, whereas the outcomes of behavior are the ways in which the behaving individual's environment is somehow different as a result of his or her behavior" (Nickols as cited in Stolovitch & Keeps, 1999, p. 4). For example, a person might know what the jitterbug is (knowledge) and be able to do a couple of steps after watching a video (behavioral change), but this does not always mean that the person's jitterbug performance will be applauded by an audience (performance, as in an outcome of that behavior).

In other words, performance is measured in terms of the *accomplishment* produced by specific knowledge and behavior. Harless (1989) provides interesting questions that help distinguish knowledge, behavior, and accomplished performance:

1. If you've stopped breathing, whom do you want to show up?

   Paramedic #1: I know how a resuscitator works.
   Paramedic #2: I know how to work a resuscitator.
   Paramedic #3: I have accomplished resuscitation before.

2. Forced to choose, whom do you want to pilot your plane?

Pilot candidate #1: I know the principles of aerodynamics.
Pilot candidate #2: They taught me the steps of flying.
Pilot candidate #3: I have accomplished many safe takeoffs,
                     flights, and landings. (pp. 36–37)

Paramedic #3 and Pilot #3, who have accomplished the tasks, are more qualified than paramedics and pilots who have not.

Engineering human performance	Human performance requires an *engineering* process. To illustrate it, Spitzer provides three fundamental theories about performance:

1. Performance will never improve by itself.
2. Once deteriorated, performance becomes increasingly resistant to improvement.
3. Performance will only stay improved if there is continuing support from the performance improvement system. (as cited in Rosenberg, 1996, pp. 372–373)

Improving human performance requires both *systematic* and *systemic* engineering approaches:

- **Systematic engineering processes.** As in most engineering situations, one of the first steps in engineering human performance is to conduct a thorough analysis of the performance, which is often referred to as a front-end analysis (Harless, 1975). The front-end analysis reveals the true nature of the performance problem. If it is a human performer-related issue, it proceeds with the steps of cause analysis, intervention selection, design, implementation, change management, and evaluation.

- **Systemic engineering processes.** While following the systematic engineering process, human performance requires a holistic view of performance factors, including the organization, the performance context and process, and the performance of individuals (Rummler & Brache, 1992).

Human performance technology model	The systematic and systemic process of engineering human performance is illustrated in the Human Performance Technology (HPT) model, as shown in Figure 18 (Van Tiem, Moseley, & Dessigner, 2004). The overall process presented in the HPT model follows the framework of the ADDIE model (consisting of the analysis, design, development, implementation, and evaluation phases). However, it puts greater emphasis on the front-end analysis phase before proceeding to the design and development phases.

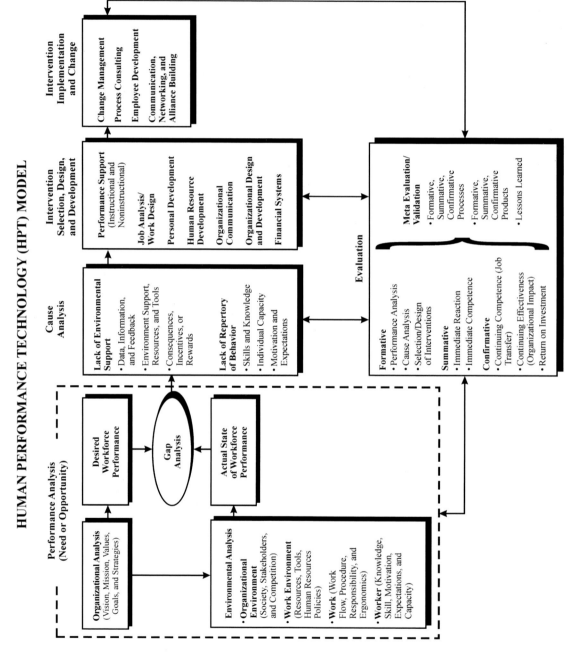

Figure 18. Human performance technology (HPT) model.

(Copyright 2004. HPT Model is from page 3 of *Fundamentals of Performance Technology*, Second Edition by D. M. Van Tiem, J. L. Moseley, & J. C. Dessinger, published by the International Society for Performance Improvement (ISPI). All rights reserved. Reprinted with permission of ISPI.)

Human Performance Technology

The beginnings of human performance technology	The field of instructional technology continued to develop during the 1950s and 1960s. As practitioners were applying systematic and systemic approaches to handling learning and performance issues, it became evident to them that instruction could not be the only solution to all problems and that they needed to look beyond the instructional system. Swanson (1999) explains it this way:

> During this postwar period, the Instructional System Development model (ISD), primarily driven from the psychological domain, gained support from the military, its host organization. A false assumption was that the ISD view of the world was directly and consciously connected to organizational performance in the private sector. It was not. And when the larger performance infrastructure of American business and industry weakened, the postwar ISD model became less viable as a way truly to identify and solve core performance problems. (pp. 3–4)

Based on this perspective, human performance technology as a field of study began to evolve from its parent field, instructional technology. As a result, the National Society for Programmed Instruction (NSPI), originally founded in 1962, changed its name to the National Society for Performance and Instruction (NSPI) in the 1970s. It changed its name again in 1995 to the International Society for Performance Improvement (Rosenberg, 1996).

Definitions of human performance technology	Different authors and practitioners define human performance technology in different ways. Their definitions altogether form a comprehensive understanding about what human performance technology is.

- Human performance technology is "a field of endeavor which seeks to bring about changes to a system in such a way that the system is improved in terms of the achievements it values" (Stolovitch, 1982, p. 16).

- Human performance technology is defined as "the process of selection, analysis, design, development, implementation, and evaluation of programs to most cost-effectively influence human behavior and accomplishment" (Harless, as cited in Geis, 1986, p. 1).

- Human performance technology is "a perspective or way of thinking about how individual and organizational performance can be enhanced" (Rosenberg, 1996, p. 390).

These definitions point out the accomplishment of performers and/or organizational improvement as the expected outcomes of practicing human performance technology.

Characteristics of human performance technology	Human performance technology as a field possesses a distinctive set of characteristics:

- Human performance technology is based on the assumption that human performance is *lawful* (Geis, 1986).

  The lawful principles used in the practice of human performance technology are derived from various fields, including behavioral and cognitive psychology, sociology, anthropology, communications, business management, and systems theory.

- Human performance technology is *empirical* (Geis, 1986).

  This means that the practice of human performance technology relies on observations and/or experiments, and decisions are made based on concrete data. For example, during the needs assessment phase, needs are determined by observing, measuring, and studying current performance levels and comparing them to the desired performance levels.

- Human performance technology is *results oriented*.

  Harless (1986) emphasizes that the fundamental principle of human performance technology is that "any intervention we prescribe and develop must produce a measurable and cost-effective change in performance on part of the target audience" (p. 106).

- Human performance technology is both *reactive* and *proactive* to situations in which human performance issues are found.

  As with instructional technology, human performance technology is practiced to (a) eliminate or reduce conditions that may impede what is considered to be desirable performance outcomes (reactive), (b) prevent such conditions from happening so that desirable performance outcomes can be achieved (proactive), or (c) improve the quality of current performance environments (reactive and proactive).

- Human performance technology uses both *systematic* and *systemic* approaches to solving human performance problems.

  Having a systemic perspective is particularly critical in practicing human performance technology, as human performance is not just produced by the performer alone; it is greatly influenced by various factors in the workplace, such as the organizational culture, the work process, the work environment, or the incentive system.

- Human performance technology is open to *various interventions* that help achieve goals (Stolovitch & Keeps, 1999).

Instruction is one of the possible interventions that can be used in the practice of human performance technology. For that reason, human performance technology as a field subsumes the field of instructional technology, although the field of human performance technology evolved from the field of instructional technology (see Figure 19).

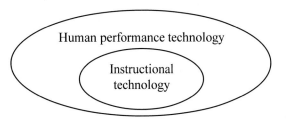

Figure 19. HPT subsumes IT.

Avoiding the hammer syndrome

The "hammer syndrome" refers to a situation where you have only a hammer in your toolbox, and everything you see appears to be a nail; you will have to use the hammer to fix everything, no matter what the problem is. As a result, the outcome might not be what you expect.

This analogy is often used to indicate that if instruction is the only method that practitioners know of, in every situation where they face a performance problem, they will try to use instruction as the solution to the problem, regardless of the cause of the problem. To avoid the hammer syndrome, practitioners should have interventions in their toolbox, including instructional and noninstructional intervention tools, and be able to know *how* to use each of them and *when* a particular tool should be used in a certain situation over another. Possible HPT interventions include the following:

- Job redesign or job reassignment
- Selection of workers with desirable knowledge, skills, and attitudes
- Culture change (selling, organizational development)
- Incentive and feedback systems
- Organizational communication
- Facilities design
- Tools design
- Education and training
- Job aids (Thiagarajan, 1984)

HPT in action

Consider the following scenario:

> Tim is the new manager of Harry's Home Hardware. When he was hired, he heard that the company was recently experiencing a drop in monthly revenue. During the first week of his employment, Tim noticed that employees often struggled to assist customers in finding the products that they needed. As he continued to observe his employees in the following weeks, he noted that it seemed to be a widespread problem. Tim decided to hold a mandatory employee training program in which he would give everyone a thorough tour of the store and conclude with a scavenger hunt activity. To ensure that employees buy into this activity, he made a list of potential negative and positive reactions his employees might have, and he made a plan to address those reactions. Then, he carried out the training. In the weeks that followed, he observed his employees and evaluated the effectiveness of the training. (Berg, Weak, & Caswell, 2006)

In this scenario, Tim assumed that the performance problem was caused by a lack of knowledge. Based on this assumption, he decided that the employees had to be trained to improve their knowledge and that the increased knowledge would help them produce better performance. However, Tim might have approached the situation differently had he followed more rigorous HPT processes. For example, Tim should have asked some of the following questions before deciding to use training as the intervention:

- What is the company's current revenue? What is the desirable level? Is the gap significant enough to worry about?
- What are the products about which employees have difficulty assisting customers? Are there common items that they have difficulty finding?
- Why do employees think they have difficulty assisting customers in finding products? Is it due to a lack of knowledge, a lack of time (too busy), or a lack of adequate stock?
- Are any types of performance support systems, such as job aids, currently available to the employees? Would employees find a job aid to be helpful?

These questions should have been asked during the performance analysis and cause analysis phases. It is possible that employees were having difficulty assisting customers in finding products, not only because they were confused about the locations of the products, but also because there were not enough employees on duty during busy hours, because the products were not clearly labeled on the shelves, and/or because the products were not in stock. In such cases, training alone would not have solved the problem. Noninstructional interventions such as job redesign/reassignment, job aids, and supply checks would also be needed.

References

Berg, S. A., Weak, K., & Caswell, C. (2006). *A hypothetical scenario: HPT needed.* Unpublished manuscript, Boise State University.

Gagné, R. M., Briggs, L. J., & Wager, W. W. (1992). *Principles of instructional design* (4th ed.). Orlando, FL: Harcourt Brace Jovanovich.

Geis, G. L. (1986). Human performance technology: An overview. In D. Brethower (Ed.), *Introduction to performance technology* (Vol. 1, pp. 1–20). Washington, D.C.: The National Society for Performance and Instruction.

Harless, J. H. (1975). *An ounce of analysis (is worth a pound of objectives): A self-instructional lesson* (3rd ed.). Newnan, GA: Harless Performance Guild, Inc.

Harless, J. H. (1986). Guiding performance with job aids. In D. Brethower (Ed.), *Introduction to performance technology* (Vol. 1, pp. 106–124). Washington, D.C.: The National Society for Performance and Instruction.

Harless, J. H. (1989, May). Wasted behavior: A confession. *Training, 26*, 35–38.

Merriam-Webster's collegiate dictionary (11th ed.). (2003). Springfield, MA: Merriam-Webster.

Rosenberg, M. (1996). Human performance technology. In R. Craig (Ed.), *The ASTD training & development handbook* (4th ed., pp. 370–393). New York: McGraw-Hill.

Rummler, G. A., & Brache, A. P. (1992). *Improving performance: How to manage the white space on the organizational chart.* San Francisco: Jossey-Bass.

Saettler, P. (1968). *A history of instructional technology.* New York: McGraw-Hill.

Shrock, S. (1995). A brief history of instructional development. In G. Anglin (Ed.), *Instructional technology: Past, present, and future* (2nd ed., pp. 11–19). Englewood, CO: Libraries Unlimited.

Stolovitch, H. (1982). Performance technology: An introduction. *Performance and Instruction, 21*(3), 16–19.

Stolovich, H., & Keeps, E. (1999). What is human performance technology? In H. Stolovich, & E. Keeps (Eds.), *Handbook of human performance technology* (2nd ed., pp. 3–23). San Francisco: Jossey-Bass.

Swanson, R. A. (1999). The foundations of performance improvement and implications for practice. In R. J. Torrace (Ed.), *Performance improvement theory and practice: Advances in developing human resources* (No. 1, pp. 1–25). San Francisco: Berrett-Koehler Communications, Inc.

Thiagarajan, S. (1984). How to avoid instruction. *Performance & Instruction, 23*(3), 10.

Van Tiem, D. M., Moseley, J. L., & Dessigner, J. C. (2004). *Fundamentals of performance technology* (2nd ed.). Washington, D. C.: The International Society for Performance Improvement.

Engineering Human Competence

Engineering Human Performance

Engineering
human
performance

Human performance technology started to be recognized as a field of study in the 1970s. There were several pioneers who helped establish the field of human performance technology. Thomas Gilbert, working with other visionaries such as Robert Mager, Joe Harless, and Geary Rummler, greatly contributed to the development of the field of human performance technology (Dean, 1997).

Perhaps one of the most important contributions that Gilbert made to the field was his help in establishing the foundational concepts of *engineering human performance*. With his theories, Gilbert emphasized the importance of using systematic, systemic, and cost-effective ways to change human behavior in order to generate accomplishments that are valued by the organization as well as the performer.

Performance
based on
accomplishment

Gilbert (1976) clarified that *performance* is different from *behavior*, and that performance should be measured based on the degree of *accomplishment*. For example, a typist's hand position on the keyboard and the tone of voice of a telephone help-desk clerk are measures of their behavior, not their accomplishment. Instead, the focus should be on measuring the typist's rate of completing error-free manuscripts and measuring the telephone help-desk clerk's accuracy in trouble-shooting and other diagnostic processes. This echoes the principle of human performance technology that *performance is not the same as behavior; it is the outcome of behavior.*

Gilbert (1976, 1978) believed that virtually all performance can be measured if we focus on *accomplishment* instead of human behavior. In other words, human competence is measured by accomplishment rather than behavior, and there are various ways to measure performance. For example, he explained that a writer's performance could be measured not only by the number of manuscripts produced, but also by the readers' satisfaction or by the number of times people cited the manuscripts.

Gilbert's
leisurely
theorems

This chapter provides an overview of Gilbert's "leisurely" theorems. Gilbert (1996) introduced four leisurely theorems in his book *Human Competence: Engineering Worthy Performance.* The first leisurely theorem is about the concept of worthy performance. The second leisurely theorem is about the concept of potential for improving performance. The third leisurely theorem is about the behavior engineering model, and the fourth leisurely theorem is about the different levels of accomplishments.

It is highly recommended that HPT practitioners read Gilbert's book *Human Competence: Engineering Worthy Performance* (1996), especially the first four chapters of the book that explain the four leisurely theorems in detail.

Thomas Gilbert's Leisurely Theorems

Thomas Gilbert (1927–1995)	Thomas Gilbert, known as *the father of human performance technology*, was a behaviorist who once worked in Skinner's laboratories. He taught at several universities and essentially created the job category of professional performance engineer. Gilbert published *Human Competence: Engineering Worthy Performance* in 1978, in which he described his leisurely theorems (including the behavior engineering model). Gilbert's work was influenced by Frederick Taylor, Kurt Lewin, and B. F. Skinner. He helped found the National Society for Programmed Instruction in the early 1960s, now known as the International Society for Performance Improvement (Dean, 1997; Gilbert, 1996).
Leisure = time + opportunity	Gilbert (1996) explained the meaning behind the term *leisurely theorems* by saying that the word *leisure* is rooted in an old French word that means "permission," which in turn implies an "opportunity" for doing something different and better, and the "time" available for doing so:

> When we are permitted a break from arduous labor, we have the opportunity to accomplish other things. The Oxford English Dictionary calls it "an opportunity afforded by freedom from occupations," and "time allowed before it is too late." . . . If (old-style) leisure is the product of time and opportunity, it is, indeed, the worthy aim of a system of performance engineering, and the one I consider to be its true purpose. (p. 11)[1]

Gilbert (1996) used the word *leisurely* as a synonym for *human capital*, the product of time and opportunity, in describing his principles of engineering human performance and improving human competence. He called those principles "leisurely theorems."

Four leisurely theorems	In his leisurely theorems, Gilbert (1976, 1996) provided foundational concepts of human performance engineering, which help HPT practitioners:

1. Understand the meaning of *worthy* performance.
2. Compare exemplary performance to typical performance, and analyze the gap between the two (that is, the potential for improving performance).
3. Diagnose areas where performance deficiencies are found, and determine how to produce worthy performance.
4. Develop a systemic perspective on evaluating the values of accomplishments.

[1] Acknowledgment: Several quotes of Thomas Gilbert included in this book are from *Human Competence: Engineering Worthy Performance* by T. Gilbert. Copyright © 1996 by the International Society for Performance Improvement. Reprinted with permission of John Wiley and Sons, Inc.

Worthy Performance

Two aspects of performance: behavior and accomplishment

Behavior is a necessary element of performance, but performance is more than exhibiting a certain behavior. According to Gilbert (1988), behavior and accomplishment are two aspects of performance: "In performance, behavior is a means; its consequence is the end" (p. 49).

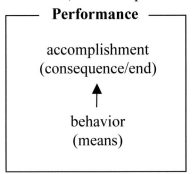

For example,

- Studying hard is a behavior. Passing an exam is an accomplishment.
- Entering customers' information into a database is a behavior. Producing accurate data entry and increasing customer satisfaction while providing timely customer support by using the database are accomplishments.

To understand the value of performance, it should be evaluated in terms of the two aspects of the performance: the behavior and its accomplishment. Below is a hypothetical scenario:

John is an assistant in your department. One of John's responsibilities is to make sure that the members of the department are aware of monthly meetings. John used to call everyone on the phone and remind them of the scheduled meeting time and place. The attendance was pretty good (over 85 percent), but calling everyone was time-consuming. It took a long time for him to get the job done.

When a new version of the company e-mail system was installed, John decided to start using the calendar feature of the system, but he needed training. You sent him to a training program and he learned how to use the electronic calendar feature. He realized that it could be an effective tool to quickly distribute information to many people. Since then, John has been using the electronic calendar system to announce meeting schedules to people in your department. As soon as he hits the "send" key to send the announcement messages, he assumes he has accomplished his task. However, after he started using the e-mail system to announce the monthly meeting, only about 50 to 60 percent of the people came to the meeting. The rest of the people later reported that they did not even learn about the meeting schedule in time, because they do not frequently check their e-mail messages.

This scenario illustrates the difference between *behavior* and *accomplishment*. John exhibited a certain behavior, but failed to produce a desirable level of accomplishment. He completed a training program and used the new electronic calendar system (his behavior), but he did not help all attendees come to the meeting (his accomplishment level). To help John improve his performance, both his behavior and his accomplishment level should be evaluated.

As another example, calling a customer, making a job aid, and writing down an order are behaviors, and a sale is an accomplishment of those behaviors. If a sale is not produced, the behaviors are seen as ineffective. This calls for an investigation to see how the outcome can be improved.

Behavior is something that you take with you and an accomplishment is something that you leave behind (Gilbert & Gilbert, 1992, p. 44).

Worthy performance

Gilbert (1996) states that "human competence is a function of worthy performance (W), which is a function of the ratio of valuable accomplishments (A) to costly behavior (B)" (p. 18). This is Gilbert's first leisurely theorem, which he expresses with the following formula:

$$W = \frac{A}{B} \text{ (p. 18)} \quad \text{or more precisely,} \quad W = f\left(\frac{A}{B}\right) \text{ (p. 26)}$$

From a performance engineering standpoint, a worthy performance index is measured by the ratio of expected valuable accomplishments (A) to the costs needed for changing behavior (B). When the worthy performance index value is smaller than 1 (i.e., the costs are greater than the value of the accomplishment), the performance is considered unworthy, and when the worthy performance index value is larger than 1, the performance is considered worthy. In other words:

- Evaluating the worthiness of performance requires measurement of both the value of an accomplishment and the costs needed for changing behavior in order to produce the valuable accomplishment.
- Performance becomes worthy when the value of an accomplishment exceeds the costs needed for changing behavior in order to produce the valuable accomplishment.

For example, in John's scenario, training was provided to him and it accounted for the cost of changing his behavior (i.e., using the new e-mail calendar system). However, his new behavior did not result in a desired level of accomplishment. Therefore, in a conceptual sense, his new performance level would not be considered *worthy*.

Gilbert (1996) explains that the first leisurely theorem is the key to a human performance engineering system and that the other theorems were constructed based on the first one.

Potential for Improving Performance

Exemplary performance vs. typical performance

Consider the following scenario in the context previously presented:

> Jane is an assistant in another department. Her role is also to announce meeting schedules for her department. The attendance rate in her department is always over 95 percent. The average attendance rate in all of the departments is about 65 percent. All other departments want their average attendance to be as high as 95 percent.

Jane's performance is called an *exemplary* performance, which Gilbert (1996) defines as "the worth of the historically best instance of the performance" (p. 30). The other departments' assistants are producing *typical* performance levels.

Exemplary performance and typical performance can be measured for *groups* as well as *individual performers*. For example, suppose that a training program was delivered to four different groups of trainees. Table 19 shows the results of a criterion-referenced test conducted at the end of the training. In this example, the exemplary performance among individuals is 100 and the exemplary performance among the groups is 93.7. The typical performance level is the average value of the 40 individual scores: 83.7.

Table 19. An Example of Exemplary Performance vs. Typical Performance

Group	A	B	C	D	Average
Individual Scores	99	*100*	98	88	—
	98	95	97	83	
	98	94	90	79	
	95	91	86	77	
	95	90	85	67	
	93	90	82	65	
	91	88	78	63	
	90	85	77	61	
	90	77	74	60	
	88	62	70	59	
Average	*93.7*	87.2	83.7	70.2	*83.7*

Potential for improving performance

According to Gilbert (1996), the potential for improving performance (PIP) is the ratio of exemplary performance (W_{ex}) to typical performance (W_t).

Typical competence is inversely proportional to the potential for improving performance (the PIP), which is the ratio of exemplary performance to typical performance. The ratio, to be meaningful, must be stated for an identifiable accomplishment, because there is no "general quality of competence" (p. 30).

This is Gilbert's second leisurely theorem. Gilbert (1996) expresses it in the following formula:

$$\mathbf{PIP} = \frac{\mathbf{W}_{ex}}{\mathbf{W}_t} \text{ (p. 30)}$$

Gilbert (1996) calls the second leisurely theorem the *Measurement Theorem*, as the PIP is "a measure of opportunity" (p. 31). For example, other assistants in John's scenario have the potential or the opportunity to improve their performance levels up to Jane's level, and the assistants' PIP is 1.46 (95 ÷ 65).

In the example presented in Table 19, the PIP of the person who scored the lowest is 1.69 (100 ÷ 59) and the PIP of Group D is 1.33 (93.7 ÷ 70.2). Since the average score is 83.7 and the highest score is 100, the average PIP is 1.19 (100 ÷ 83.7).

While Gilbert's first leisurely theorem helps practitioners conceptualize the fundamental "dimensions" required for engineering human competence (i.e., the value of accomplishments and the costs for changing behavior), his second leisurely theorem helps them in different ways:

- It helps practitioners understand that human competence is *measured and compared based on performance* instead of the individuals themselves. "People are not competent; performance is. People have opportunities, which the PIP can express with precision and validity" (p. 31).

- It helps practitioners view *a performance gap as a potential for performance improvement,* rather than as a problem to solve. The smaller the PIP of a performer, the harder it is to help the performer close the PIP, as it would mean that the typical performance level is close to the exemplary performance level. It may also mean that they are in a very competitive group. The larger a performer's PIP is, the greater potential for improvement the performer has.

- This second leisurely theorem also helps practitioners understand that the human performance engineering process is a *dynamic process*, as "the PIP is a 'dynamic' measure, because new exemplary standards can always be set" (p. 31).

The measurement of a PIP indicates the amount of potential for improving performance, but it does not provide information on economical ways to reduce the PIP. Gilbert states that it is the manager's responsibility to *engineer* the work environment as well as the performer's behavior in order to help reduce a large PIP. His third leisurely theorem, the behavior engineering model, explains how to do this.

Behavior Engineering Model

Six factors in the behavior engineering model

Let's go back to John's story. He changed his behavior and started using the electronic calendar system, but he did not produce a high level of accomplishment. Even with the new calendar system and after finishing the training program, John's performance level decreased. So, what went wrong?

According to Gilbert (1996), it would take more than a new instrument or new skills to improve performance. There are six components that are necessary for behavior to occur. Three of them are environmental supports (**E**) and the other three are the performer's repertory of behavior (**P**) (see Table 20).

Table 20. Six Factors in the Behavior Engineering Model

	Information	**Instrumentation**	**Motivation**
Environmental Supports	1. Data	2. Instruments	3. Incentives
Person's Repertory of Behavior	4. Knowledge	5. Capacity	6. Motives

Note. From *Human competence: Engineering worthy performance* (p. 88) by T. Gilbert. Copyright © 1996, 2006 by the International Society for Performance Improvement. Reprinted with permission of John Wiley & Sons, Inc.

Gilbert (1996) states that all six components are necessary to cause a behavior.

$$(B = P + E) \text{ therefore, } W = \frac{A}{P + E} \text{ (p. 76)}$$

This is Gilbert's third leisurely theorem, also known as the *behavior engineering model*.

Gilbert (1996) also calls the third theorem the *Management Theorem*, because from a management viewpoint, it helps identify the causes of competence and incompetence. Incompetence is ultimately caused by poor management of the six components:

> For any given accomplishment, a deficiency in performance always has as its immediate cause a deficiency in a behavior repertory (P), or in the environment that supports the repertory (E), or in both. But its ultimate cause will be found in a deficiency of the management system (M). (p. 76)

In John's case, he has a new electronic calendar system (instrument), and he knows how to schedule the meetings and make announcements (knowledge). He is capable of using the system (capacity) and is willing to use the new electronic calendar system to complete his task (motive). However, he is not producing a desired performance. What might be missing? The data seems to be missing. He might have assumed that announcing the schedule was all he had to do, when in fact, his role was to announce the schedule *and* to ensure that everybody was aware of the meeting schedule. Also, if he is rewarded for his *behavior* of using the electronic calendar system but is not evaluated on his *accomplishment*, he is receiving the wrong incentive. The lack of data and the inappropriate incentive could be the reasons for John's potential for improving performance.

Engineering from human incompetence to human competence	Human behavior can be engineered to result in either competence or incompetence. Through analysis techniques such as observations, interviews, surveys, and extant data reviews, HPT practitioners would be able to reveal factors that likely create human incompetence and determine recommendations for engineering human competence and improving the situation.

What follows are hypothetical examples of methods that would likely create human incompetence and examples of alternative methods for engineering human competence, using John's scenario.

Methods that Would Likely Create Human Incompetence

Data:
- Do not tell John that he is not producing a desirable performance level.
- Tell him that his work is complete, as long as he uses the new e-mail calendar system.
- Do not provide him with updated telephone directory information.

Instruments:
- Do not install a new e-mail calendar system on his computer.
- Remove the e-mail calendar system from his computer, as he is not using it effectively. Force him to use the telephone instead.
- Do not worry about upgrading his computer system.

Incentives:
- Allow him to attend training only after work hours or during weekends, as he should be expected to have the professional knowledge.
- Give him more work to do without rewards whenever he produces good performance.

Knowledge:
- Send him to a training program. It will be less expensive, even though it teaches a different electronic calendar software program.
- Expect him to teach himself how to use the new electronic calendar system.

Capacity:
- Since he is knowledgeable in using the new e-mail and electronic calendar system and seems to be good at using computers, assign him the task of maintaining the network system in the company as well.

Motives:
- Maintain a work environment that will likely cause low job satisfaction levels (dirty, messy, noisy, no promotion, etc.).
- Evaluate his performance based on arbitrarily set criteria each time.

Alternative Methods for Engineering Human Competence

Data:
- Tell John that he is not producing a desirable performance level, and discuss with him how he can improve his performance level.
- Tell him that his job responsibilities include announcing the meeting schedules and making sure that participants are aware of the meeting schedule.
- Provide him with updated telephone directory information.

Instruments:
- Install a new e-mail calendar system on his computer.
- If necessary, upgrade his computer system so that the new software will run effectively.

Incentives:
- Allow him to attend training during his work hours as part of his professional development plan.
- Recognize and reward his good performance.

Knowledge:
- Send him to a training program that helps him improve his skills in using the new electronic calendar system.
- Provide job aids to support his performance, as needed.

Capacity:
- Adjust his workload to give him enough time to complete his tasks while he is still learning to use the new e-mail calendar system effectively.

Motives:
- Provide reinforcement in public, and offer personal feedback for improvement privately.
- Encourage him to seek career development opportunities.

Using behavior engineering model as a diagnostic tool

When managers detect a large amount of PIP and believe it is critical to close the gap, they should ask themselves questions such as: Why are some employees not performing as well as the exemplary performer? What caused the PIP? How can I help reduce the PIP? What can be done to help employees produce *worthy performance*?

According to Gilbert (1996), the behavioral engineering model can be used as a *diagnostic tool* to investigate the causes of the performance gap and to determine effective and efficient solutions for closing the gap. When diagnosing where the deficiencies in behavior occur, Gilbert suggests taking the steps in the following order:

Data → Instruments → Incentives → Knowledge → Capacity → Motives

By following the sequence, practitioners attempt to answer questions such as:

1. (Data) Do typical performers know what they are expected to do?
2. (Instruments) Do they have appropriate tools to do their job?
3. (Incentives) Are they rewarded for doing a good job?
4. (Knowledge) Do they have enough knowledge to do their job?
5. (Capacity) Are they capable of performing, or are they ready to do the job?
6. (Motives) Are they motivated to perform the job?

The behavior engineering model helps practitioners determine where the causes of a performance problem are and which strategies will produce the most worthy performance from an engineering perspective—that is, to achieve *the greatest improvement* in accomplishment *at the lowest cost* for changing behavior. In other words, **where is the greatest leverage?**

Figure 20 below explains the conceptual framework of the behavior engineering model.

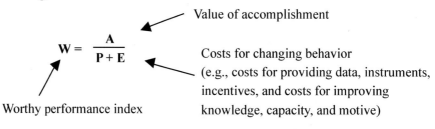

Figure 20. The conceptual framework of the behavior engineering model.

Diffusion
of effects

The behavior engineering model is not just a tool that helps one observe human work behavior in a *systematic* way. It also helps maximize the overall effects of selected interventions in a *systemic* way. This is called the *diffusion of effects*. Gilbert (1996) explains that "there is no way to alter one condition of behavior without having at least some effect on another aspect—often, a considerable effect. And usually it is difficult, if not impossible, to determine the degree of the diffusion of the effects" (p. 94).

Some practitioners may try to find a solution that deals with each of the causes. For example, if a performer does not have enough knowledge, training can be an appropriate solution. If a performer does not have a necessary tool, provide one. Gilbert does not disapprove of this "matching" method, but he argues that practitioners should be able to anticipate that altering the condition in one area could have some side effects on other areas.

When taking this systemic approach to selecting intervention(s), it is important to be aware that the selected intervention(s) can produce both positive and negative side effects. For example, providing a new instrument can be seen as an incentive as well, which may motivate performers (positive side effects). But having to use a new sophisticated instrument might create a new knowledge gap, which can require additional training, or it can be over their capacity (negative side effects). These possible positive and negative side effects are illustrated in Figure 21 (also see Chyung, 2005).

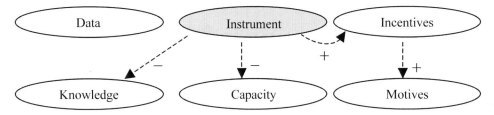

Figure 21. An example illustrating the diffusion of effects.

The fourth
leisurely
theorem

In his fourth leisurely theorem, Gilbert (1996) states that "we can view human accomplishments at several levels of generality, and the values we assign to these accomplishments at each level will be derived from the level just above them" (p. 112).

For example, let's say that a pharmaceutical company has developed a new drug that helps reduce cholesterol and that this product has helped generate substantial profits for the company. When considering the severe side effects of the drug on the overall health of the patients (i.e., the impact on the societal level, which is a level above the organizational level), a different level of value could be assigned to the company's accomplishment. The application of Gilbert's fourth leisurely theorem can be better understood within the organizational elements model (see Chapter 9).

As shown in Figure 22, Gilbert's method of measuring a PIP value falls into the gap analysis phase. His method of using the BEM as a diagnostic tool falls into the cause analysis phase. The BEM, with the idea of the diffusion of effects, also facilitates the process of selecting the most cost-effective interventions during the intervention selection phase.

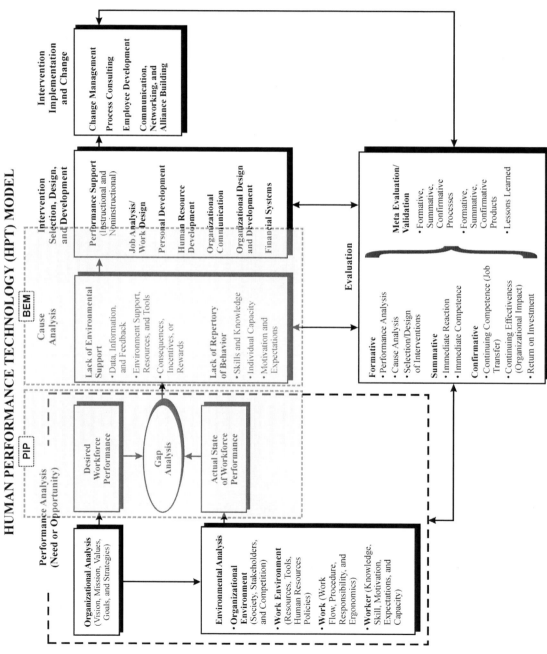

Figure 22. The use of PIP and BEM in the HPT model: Adapted from human performance technology (HPT) model.

References

Chyung, S. Y. (2005). Human performance technology: From Taylor's scientific management to Gilbert's behavior engineering model. *Performance Improvement Journal, 44*(1), 23–28.

Dean, P. J. (1997). Thomas F. Gilbert, Ph.D.: Engineering performance with or without training. In P. J. Dean, & D. E. Ripley (Eds.), *Performance improvement pathfinders: Models for organizational learning systems* (Vol. 1, pp. 45–64). Silver Spring, MD: The International Society for Performance Improvement.

Gilbert, T. F. (1976, November). Training: The $100 billion opportunity. *Training and Development*, 3–8.

Gilbert, T. F. (1978). *Human competence: Engineering worthy performance.* New York: McGraw-Hill.

Gilbert, T. F. (1988, July). Measuring the potential for performance improvement. *Training, 25*, 49–52.

Gilbert, T. F. (1996). *Human competence: Engineering worthy performance* (Tribute ed.). Washington, D.C.: The International Society for Performance Improvement.

Gilbert, T. F., & Gilbert, M. B. (1992). Potential contributions of performance science to education. *Journal of Applied Behavior Analysis, 25*(1), 43–49.

Chapter

8

Front-End Analysis

Front-End Analysis

The early stage
of an analysis

In the analysis phase, a series of analyses are conducted before reaching a conclusion about the most appropriate interventions to address a performance issue. The term *front-end analysis* is often used to refer to this phase.

Harless (1973) explains that front-end analysis is a procedure for asking various questions up front to analyze performance issues and to determine effective interventions. Terms such as *needs assessment, needs analysis,* and *performance analysis* are used as synonyms, but different authors explain the terms slightly differently. For example:

- The term *needs assessment* is often used to refer to a series of analyses that are conducted up front. But it can also be used to refer to a *training needs assessment* (Rossett, 1987), conducted "when the instructional technologist is trying to respond to a request for assistance" (Rossett, 1995, p. 184).

- A *needs assessment* is also "the process for identifying needs and placing them in priority order on the basis of what it costs to meet the need, versus what it costs to ignore it" (Kaufman, 1994, p. 14). This view emphasizes the assessment of performance-oriented needs and is open to many possible interventions (instead of assuming training as the pre-selected intervention).

- Different authors define *needs analysis* differently. According to Kaufman (1994), a needs analysis is "the process of determining the reasons and causes for a need so that appropriate interventions may be identified and later selected" (p. 14). According to Molenda, Pershing, and Reigeluth (1996), a needs analysis includes the steps of determining performance deficiencies and identifying the source(s) of those deficiencies.

- *Performance analysis* is the process of "determining the organization's performance requirements in light of its objectives and its capabilities" (Rosenberg, 1996, p. 377). Performance analysis is conducted to reveal a performance opportunity or problem, and it may lead to a lengthier training needs assessment if instruction is identified as a solution (Rossett, 1999).

Front-end
analysis

This chapter explains the process of front-end analysis as Harless defines it, and presents a case study. The term *front-end analysis* will be used to refer to the procedure that includes phases of performance analysis, cause analysis, and intervention selection, as presented in the HPT model.

Joe Harless's Front-End Analysis

Front-end
analysis vs.
back-end
analysis

Joe Harless is credited with coining the term *front-end analysis* in his book *An Ounce of Analysis Is Worth a Pound of Objectives*, originally published in 1970 (Harless, 1975). The purpose of conducting a front-end analysis (FEA) can be clearly explained when it is compared to the practice of conducting a back-end analysis—that is, an evaluation. As practitioners start recognizing a problem associated with instructional outcomes, they might ask themselves, "Why didn't training produce the performance that we expected to see?"

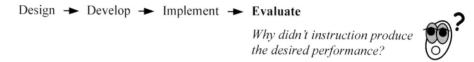

Design → Develop → Implement → **Evaluate**

Why didn't instruction produce the desired performance?

Several possible hypotheses can be formulated:

> Perhaps the training objectives were not relevant to the trainee's real-world needs. Perhaps the training activities did not simulate the real world as closely as possible. Perhaps there was something in the environment that prevented the trainees from exhibiting the learned behavior on the job. (Harless, 1988, p. 43)

Or perhaps training should not have been delivered in the first place, because it was not an appropriate solution to the performance problem. To avoid providing unnecessary training, practitioners should conduct a front-end analysis and ask various questions that help determine the nature of the performance problem and find root causes. In fact, Harless (1973) argues that "FEA seeks to avoid instruction whenever possible" (p. 239).

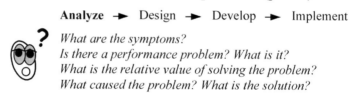

Analyze → Design → Develop → Implement

What are the symptoms?
Is there a performance problem? What is it?
What is the relative value of solving the problem?
What caused the problem? What is the solution?

However, *front-end analysis* and *evaluation* are both important. By conducting front-end analysis as well as evaluation, we have a complete cycle through the ADDIE steps. As shown in Figure 23, evaluation is conducted to reveal whether or not the performance problems identified during a front-end analysis have been solved, and the evaluation data will be used during the next phase of front-end analysis.

Analyze → Design → Develop → Implement → **Evaluate**

Feedback

Figure 23. Relationship of front-end analysis and evaluation.

Smart Questions to Ask during Front-End Analysis

About money,
first and
foremost

Harless (1973) explains that the purpose of conducting a front-end analysis is to ask a series of "smart questions" in order to prevent spending money on unnecessary activities, to come up with the most appropriate solution(s), and to produce desired performance outcomes:

> Front-end analysis is about money, first and foremost. It's about how to spend money in ways that will be most beneficial to the organization and the performers in that organization. It is also about *avoiding* spending money on silly things like instruction when there is no instructional problem; or training everybody in everything when you can get by with training fewer people in a few things; or flying lots of trainees in for a course when a send-out checklist would do. (p. 229)

> Front-end analysis is problem solving applied to human perform-ance—a series of analytical and decision-making steps that lead to plans for overcoming deficiencies in human performance. It is all the smart questions that a manager, educator, trainer, and consultant should ask before deciding what specific solution to develop for a performance problem. (p. 231)

Harless (1973) lists 13 major "smart questions" to be asked during a front-end analysis:

1. Do we have a problem?
2. Do we have a performance problem?
3. How will we know when the problem is solved?
4. What is the performance problem?
5. Should we allocate resources to solve it?
6. What are the possible causes of the problem?
7. What evidence bears on each possibility?
8. What is the probable cause?
9. What general solution type is indicated?
10. What are the alternative subclasses of solutions?
11. What are the costs, effects, and development times of each solution?
12. What are the constraints?
13. What are the overall goals? (p. 231)

Asking these smart questions helps organizations (1) spend money on performance problems that are *worth solving*, (2) thoroughly investigate the causes of the problems, and (3) determine the most cost-effective solutions. The front-end analysis process does not assume instruction to be a solution to all types of performance problems.

FEA within the HPT model

The front-end analysis procedure is aligned with the first three major steps in the HPT model, as shown in Table 21 and Figure 24:

Table 21. FEA "Smart Questions" to be Asked in the HPT Model

The HPT Model (Van Tiem, Moseley, and Dessinger, 2004)	**Front-End Analysis "Smart Questions"** (Harless, 1973, p. 231)
Performance analysis	1. Do we have a problem? 2. Do we have a performance problem? 3. How will we know when the problem is solved? 4. What is the performance problem? 5. Should we allocate resources to solve it?
Cause analysis	6. What are the possible causes of the problem? 7. What evidence bears on each possibility? 8. What is the probable cause?
Intervention selection, design, and development	9. What general solution type is indicated? 10. What are the alternative subclasses of solutions? 11. What are the costs, effects, and development times of each solution? 12. What are the constraints? 13. What are the overall goals? (The intervention design and development steps are not part of FEA)
Intervention implementation and change	(Not part of FEA)
Evaluation	(Not part of FEA)

Two of the 13 questions help practitioners project the relative value of investing money for addressing performance problems (i.e., the return on investment concept). They are explained below:

- Question #5: *Should we allocate resources to solve it?* This question addresses the degree of importance in solving the identified performance problem. When the problem is too trivial to spend money on, the front-end analysis will end in this step.

- Question #11: *What are the costs, effects, and development times of each solution?* This question focuses on the cost-effectiveness of each proposed solution. The best solution is not always the most cost-effective one; if it is too costly to implement, it will not be a feasible solution.

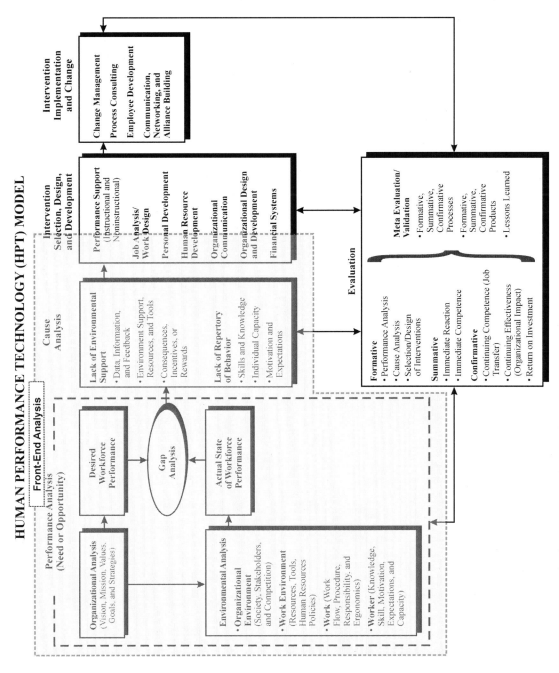

Figure 24. The front-end analysis phase in the HPT model: Adapted from human performance technology (HPT) model.

Ishikawa's cause-and-effect analysis and behavior engineering model

Methods that can be used during a cause analysis include Ishikawa's cause-and-effect analysis, as well as Gilbert's behavior engineering model.

Cause analysis	6. What are the possible causes of the problem? 7. What evidence bears on each possibility? 8. What is the probable cause?

A Japanese scholar, Kaoru Ishikawa, developed the cause-and-effect analysis (Ishikawa, 1985). This analysis, using a fishbone-looking diagram, is also known as the *fishbone analysis*. The diagram consists of three sections: the head, the main bones, and the small bones (see Figure 25). The following steps are taken when using a cause-and-effect analysis:

1. The effect or problem is stated in the head area.
2. Several categories of causes are labeled at the end of the main bones.
3. Root causes, often identified by asking a "why" question multiple times, are listed in the small bones coming off of the main bones.

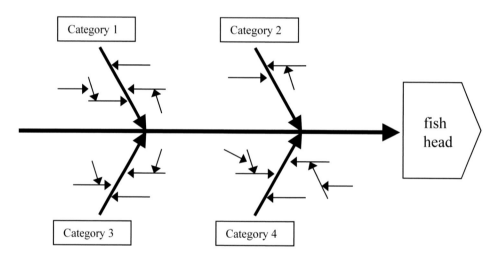

Figure 25. A fishbone diagram.

Examples of categories that can be used to construct the main bones are
- man (people), materials, machines, and methods;
- manpower, management, materials, and methods;
- people, policies, procedures, and plant.
  (Rothwell, Hohne, & King, 2000)

In human performance engineering situations, the categorization of the causes can be made with the six cells in Gilbert's behavioral engineering model: the three environmental factors (data, instruments, and incentives), and the three personal factors of knowledge, capacity, and motives (Rothwell, 1996). The PIP would be stated in the head area.

For example, consider the following hypothetical situation:

> The new employees of a production team at a semiconductor manufacturing company produce wafers without imperfection 76 percent of the time. The exemplary performance is to produce wafers without imperfection 99 percent of the time. The team wants to investigate the causes of the performance gap.

The new employees' potential for improving performance is 1.30 (99 ÷ 76). Figure 26 is an example of a cause-and-effect analysis using the six cells in Gilbert's behavior engineering model as the main categories:

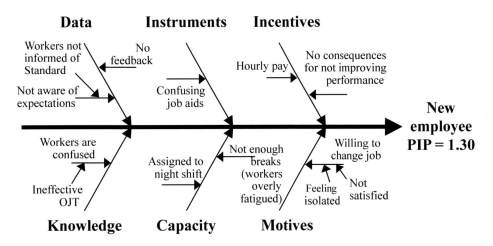

[Environmental support]

[Person's repertory of behavior]

Figure 26. A cause-and-effect analysis with BEM categories.

Once the cause-and-effect analysis is done, you can select from several interventions to improve the new employees' performance:

1. Data: provide clearly defined performance standards and feedback
2. Instruments: revise the job aids
3. Incentives: provide bonus, based on improved performance
4. Knowledge: provide structured OJT; provide guidelines to the trainers
5. Capacity: allow more breaks
6. Motives: anticipate positive diffusion of effects from other interventions, and revisit this issue in three months' time

Front-End Analysis: A Case Study

FEA in action (Lambert, 2003)	This is a hypothetical front-end analysis conducted at a mail-order retailer of photography equipment and accessories.
	Background: The company recently received an increased number of complaints from customers who ordered cameras but did not receive all the relevant support materials that should have been shipped with the cameras. These materials consist of instructional manuals for the camera and accessories, a registration form, a return-policy document, a warranty document, etc. Customers who did not receive these materials called the company's call center to complain or to ask questions that could have been answered if they had been provided with the instructions and other standard materials. Also, a new federal code will require the company to provide customers with the materials. Compliance with the new federal code is voluntary at the present time, but it will become mandatory within a couple of years.
1. Do we have a problem?	A high percentage of customers are receiving wrong, partial, or no support materials for their camera and accessories. The call center receives a large number of customer questions and complaints. When customers do not receive support materials, it also means that the company is not in compliance with the federal code. *Conclusion:* Yes, we have a problem.
2. Do we have a performance problem?	The following performance-related issues are associated with this situation: • Salespersons enter the camera order and other information into the system when receiving the order. • Then, the system issues tickets to the Distribution Center for employees to process the order. • The Distribution Center employees should then follow the tickets to manually place the appropriate support materials into the box and send them to the shipping department. *Conclusion:* Yes, we have a (human) performance problem.
3. How will we know when the problem is solved?	When the problem is solved, 1) There will be a reduction in customer complaints to the call center. 2) There will be a reduction in customer calls to the call center for questions that can be answered by the missing support materials. 3) The company will achieve federal code compliance.

| 4. What is the performance problem? | *General statement:* Customers are not satisfied because they were not given the necessary support materials when they purchased a camera. |
| | *Root problem:* The Distribution Center is not shipping all of the correct support materials to the customer along with their camera. |

| 5. Should we allocate resources to solve it? | It is important to improve customer satisfaction and achieve federal code compliance. If not handled properly, it will cause low customer satisfaction, which will in turn result in our losing customers and revenue, and eventually receiving some penalty from the federal government in the future. |
| | *Conclusion:* Yes, we should allocate resources to solve it. |

6. What are the possible causes of the problem?	Several possible causes of the problem were proposed:
	1) A system error can occur while tagging support materials at the time of purchase and wrong identifiers are entered.
	2) There are many support materials to choose from, and many contain similar information, which can be confusing to workers.
	3) Due to the high employee turnover rate, some of the new employees might be under-trained.
	4) Some boxes might be bypassing the support materials station before they are shipped to customers.

7. What evidence bears on each possibility?	Based on interviews with the Distribution Center supervisors and employees, data obtained from the Distribution Center employee survey, and the Ticketing system audit reports, it was found that:
	1) There was no evidence that support materials were tagged incorrectly in the system and wrong identifiers were assigned.
	2) Some of the Distribution Center employees were confused by similar support materials for different camera models and accessories.
	3) Some of the new employees had difficulty distinguishing different support materials from one another.
	4) Tracking records show that some boxes did bypass the support materials station.

8. What is the probable cause?	It was concluded that:
	1) It is easy for employees to get confused by the large number of support materials with similar identifiers, which can lead to human error.
	2) New employees lack knowledge required for the job.
	3) Some boxes bypass the support materials station.

9. What general solution type is indicated?	Two options were suggested: *Option A:* Provide guidance or support in how to tell which support materials go with what product. *Option B:* Redesign the workflow and ensure that no boxes bypass the support materials station.
10. What are the alternative (specific) subclasses of solutions?	Here are the detailed plans for the suggested options: *Option A:* 1) Provide job aids and posters as visual cues to help workers recognize correct support materials. 2) Analyze existing training to determine shortfalls, and then correct the training. Reduce the amount of classroom training, and increase the amount of hands-on on-the-job training (OJT) to new employees for recognizing manual identifiers and then retrieving the correct materials. *Option B:* 1) Provide workflow job aids and posters for routing boxes through the support materials station prior to shipping. 2) Regularly check the tracking records and correct errors.
11. What are the costs, effects, and development times of each solution?	*Option A:* It is possible to implement this option in a relatively short amount of time. The use of job aids is particularly cost-effective and can produce immediate effects on reducing human errors. However, the OJT is costly. Experienced employees who provide OJT are taken away from their work. *Option B:* The cost is low, and it can be implemented immediately.
12. What are the constraints?	*Option A:* There are many manuals that look alike. There is a concern that problems will still occur. The Distribution Center employee turnover might continue to be high. *Option B:* The tracking records should be manually checked.
13. What are the overall goals?	The following goals are set by the company: 1) Fewer than 5 percent of customers will receive wrong, partial, or none of the correct support materials for their camera and accessories. 2) Fewer than 5 percent of call center calls will involve complaints about missing information or questions that would have been answered had the support materials been sent. 3) The company will achieve compliance with the new federal code.

References

Harless, J. (1973). An analysis of front-end analysis. *Improving Human Performance: A Research Quarterly, 4,* 229–244.

Harless, J. (1975). *An ounce of analysis (Is worth a pound of objectives): A self-instructional lesson* (3rd ed.). Newnan, GA: Harless Performance Guild.

Harless, J. (1988, July). Front-end analysis. *Training,* 43–45.

Ishikawa, K. (1985). *Guide to quality control* (2nd rev. ed.). Tokyo: Asian Productivity Organization.

Kaufman, R. (1994). A needs assessment audit. *Performance & Improvement, 33*(2), 14–16.

Lambert, J. (2003). *Front-end analysis conducted at a mail-order photographic retailer.* Unpublished manuscript, Boise State University.

Molenda, M., Pershing, J., & Reigeluth, C. (1996). Designing instructional systems. In R. Craig (Ed.), *The ASTD training & development handbook* (4th ed., pp. 266–293). New York: McGraw-Hill.

Rosenberg, M. (1996). Human performance technology. In R. Craig (Ed.), *The ASTD training & development handbook* (4th ed., pp. 370–393). New York: McGraw-Hill.

Rossett, A. (1987). *Training needs assessment.* Englewood, NJ: Educational Technology Publications.

Rossett, A. (1995). Needs assessment. In G. Anglin (Ed.), *Instructional technology: Past, present, and future* (2nd ed., pp. 183–196). Englewood, CO: Libraries Unlimited.

Rossett, A. (1999). *First things fast: A handbook for performance analysis.* San Francisco: Jossey-Bass, Pfeiffer.

Rothwell, W. J. (1996). Section 3. Future forces. In W. J. Rothwell, *ASTD models for human performance improvement* (pp. 11–15). Alexandria, VA: The American Society for Training and Development.

Rothwell, W. J., Hohne, C. K., & King, S. B. (2000). *Human performance improvement: Building practitioner competence.* Houston, TX: Gulf Publishing Company.

Van Tiem, D. M., Moseley, J. L., & Dessigner, J. C. (2004). *Fundamentals of performance technology* (2nd ed.). Washington, D. C.: The International Society for Performance Improvement.

Chapter

9

Systemic Organizational Elements

System Thinking

System analysis through system thinking

sys·tem \\'sis-təm\ *n*

> a regularly interacting or interdependent group of items forming a unified whole <a number ~>: as (1) : a group of interacting bodies under the influence of related forces <a gravitational ~> (2) : an assemblage of substances that is in or tends to equilibrium <a thermodynamic ~>

(Merriam-Webster's Collegiate Dictionary, 2003, p. 1269)

Roger Kaufman and his associates advocate *system thinking* in HPT practice. They view not just the organization itself but also the entire society as the whole system, and they argue that various elements in the system should work together to accomplish what both the society and the organization value.

Elements in a system are interrelated, rather than independent from each other. A *system analysis* is "the procedure for identifying the elements, interrelationships, resources, and restraints of the different subsystems" (Kaufman & Thiagarajan, 1987, p. 129). Therefore, several authors explain that conducting a system analysis requires system thinking:

> System (not systems) thinking looks at the whole, and then the parts, as well as the relationship and connections among the parts. It is the opposite of reductionism (that is, the idea that something is simply the sum of its parts). After all, a collection of parts that are not connected is not a system. (Kaufman, Oakley-Browne, Watkins, & Leigh, 2003, p. 60)

These authors point out that *system* thinking is different from *systems* thinking. They explain that system thinking looks at the sum total of parts that are interdependently working together to achieve their shared goals, whereas systems thinking focuses on individual subsystems in a system. However, taking a holistic view of subcomponents in order to achieve the goal of the entire system is emphasized in both terms.

Interrelated organizational elements

This chapter provides an overview of the organizational elements model, which identifies five elements of a system and the interrelationships among them. This model is a helpful tool for strategic planning and systemic needs assessment. To solve *systemic* problems, long-term *systemic* solutions should be sought out (Banathy, 1992). The model can also be used as a systemic evaluation tool, along with Kirkpatrick's four-level model of evaluation.

Roger Kaufman's Organizational Elements Model

Means and ends   Performance technologists use various means in order to achieve desired end-results. The holistic perspective of a system helps prevent fragmented, piecemeal types of interventions and accomplishes "worthwhile ends" for all stakeholders involved. In HPT practice, success largely relies on clearly differentiating means and ends. According to Kaufman (1972, 2000):

- Means are what the organization uses and does.
- Ends are what the organization produces.

Different end-results occur when the organization selects and utilizes effective means vs. ineffective means.

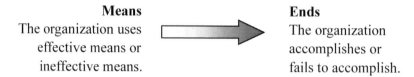

Means
The organization uses effective means or ineffective means.

Ends
The organization accomplishes or fails to accomplish.

Suppose that an engineering consulting company has decided to implement a company-wide e-learning project to increase efficiency and effectiveness in engineers' learning and performance. As shown in Figure 27, means include raw materials that the company uses and processes, and ends are the results that the company will achieve by using the means.

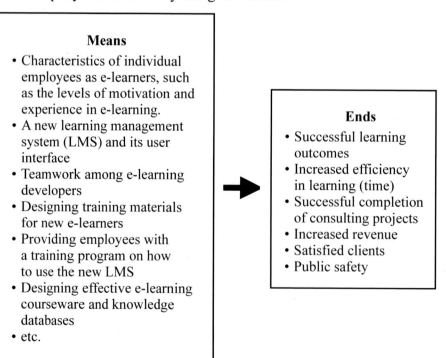

Means
- Characteristics of individual employees as e-learners, such as the levels of motivation and experience in e-learning.
- A new learning management system (LMS) and its user interface
- Teamwork among e-learning developers
- Designing training materials for new e-learners
- Providing employees with a training program on how to use the new LMS
- Designing effective e-learning courseware and knowledge databases
- etc.

Ends
- Successful learning outcomes
- Increased efficiency in learning (time)
- Successful completion of consulting projects
- Increased revenue
- Satisfied clients
- Public safety

Figure 27. An example of means and ends.

Organizational elements model

Kaufman (1979, 1981, 1988, 1992a, 1992b, 2000) conceptualized different types of means and different levels of ends, and developed a model called the *organizational elements model (OEM)*. Kaufman (2000) explains that in the OEM, the total system is described with five elements (inputs, processes, products, outputs, and outcomes), which are categorized into means and ends.

More specifically:

- An organization uses various *inputs* and *processes* as its organizational efforts to achieve a goal. Inputs are "raw materials or resources" and processes are "methods or activities." For example, the engineering consulting company may need to hire a new e-learning specialist. A "new e-learning specialist" is an input and "hiring a new e-learning specialist" is a process. Kaufman (1988) explains that one way to tell the difference between an input and a process is to look for an "-ing" in the word (e.g., hiring, managing, learning, or sharing, which are processes).

- In the OEM, there are two types of organizational results: *products* that are accomplishments that individual performers or small groups of performers produce (micro-level results), and *outputs* are accomplishments that the organization as a whole produces (macro-level results). For example, the successful completion of an engineering consulting project is a product, and the increased revenue and the satisfaction of the client because of the successful completion of the project are outputs.

- Another type of results in the OEM is *outcomes* that are the results produced beyond the organization—that is, what the society will get (mega-level results). For example, because of a successful consulting project on structural engineering, safe materials are chosen for constructing a building, which will improve public safety.

These five elements are the main categories in the OEM. The relationship among the three levels of results is illustrated in Figure 28.

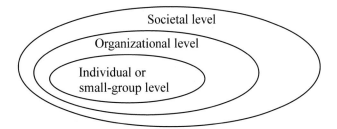

Figure 28. Three levels of results.

Different Levels of Need

Strategic planning for different levels of results

Kaufman (2000) emphasizes that strategic planning should focus on three different result levels of a system: a micro level, a macro level, and a mega level. He explains that it should start with a needs assessment at the mega level (outcomes), which leads to a needs assessment at the macro level (outputs), which in turn leads to a needs assessment at the micro level (products). Then finally, appropriate inputs and processes can be determined.

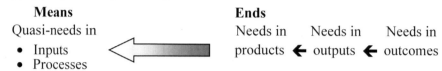

For example, the hypothetical situation of the company-wide e-learning initiative in an engineering consulting company can be explained in a more structured way with the five elements, as shown in Figure 29. The solid-line arrows indicate the strategic planning process, whereas the dotted-line arrows indicate the process of results.

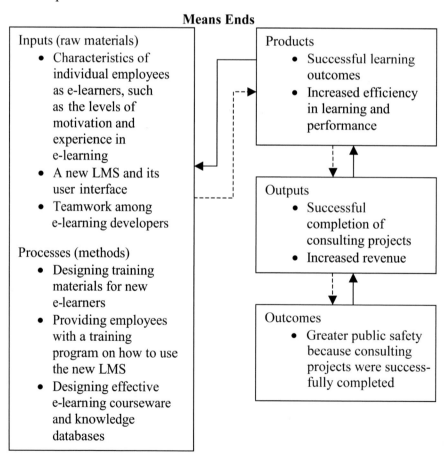

Figure 29. An example of five elements based on the OEM.

Micro, macro, and mega levels of needs

Needs are the gaps between "what should be" and "what is" in *end results*, not in means: "A needs assessment identifies gaps in results, places them in order of priority, and selects the most important for closure or reduction" (Watkins & Kaufman, 1996, p. 13). One might say, "We *need* a new computer" or "We *need* to use a different management style." However, a new computer or a different management style is a means, rather than an end result. Gaps in means such as the gap between "We don't have a new computer" and "We have a new computer" are "quasi-needs" (Kaufman, 2000; Watkins & Kaufman, 1996).

Since there are three levels of results in the OEM, three different levels of needs are analyzed when conducting needs assessments based on the OEM:

1. The mega-level need (gap)   = [what should be] – [what is]
2. The macro-level need (gap)   = [what should be] – [what is]
3. The micro-level need (gap)   = [what should be] – [what is]

For example, consider the following hypothetical scenario:

1. The mega-level gap:

    *   What should be: The regional engineering industry must employ 200 engineers who are knowledgeable in nanotechnology.
    *   What is: Currently, only 130 engineers working in the regional engineering industry are knowledgeable in nanotechnology.
    *   The gap: 70 engineers who are knowledgeable in nanotechnology

2. The macro-level gap:

    *   What should be: The engineering school in the region should graduate 65 engineers a year.
    *   What is: Currently, only 52 engineers graduate a year.
    *   The gap: 13 engineering graduates

3. The micro-level gap:

    *   What should be: Over 97 percent of engineering students should pass the required courses in nanotechnology.
    *   What is: Currently, about 89 percent of engineering students are passing the required courses in nanotechnology.
    *   The gap: Approximately 8 percent of engineering students are not passing the required courses in nanotechnology.

As shown in the scenario, the OEM structure helps an organization (in this case, the engineering school) conduct strategic planning that not only facilitates the process of setting up clear goals and effective strategies for the organization, but also helps align the organizational vision and mission with the needs of the surrounding community.

Systemic analysis of contributing factors

The OEM structure can also be utilized as a framework for conducting a *systemic* cause analysis. For example, using the previously presented hypothetical scenario, a simplified systemic cause analysis is illustrated in Figure 30. A systemic cause analysis helps practitioners recognize that means and ends are *relative* terms; that is, micro-level end results become *means* to achieving macro-level end results, which also become *means* to achieving mega-level end results. In other words, causes to a mega-level performance problem can be found in macro-level results, and causes to a macro-level performance problem can be found in micro-level results.

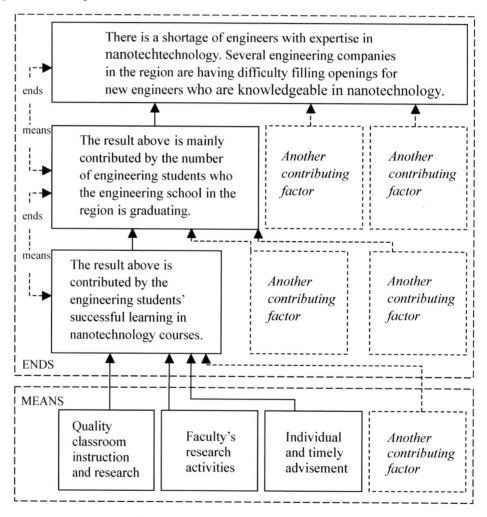

Figure 30. A systemic cause analysis.

Kaufman's OEM and Kirkpatrick's four-level model of evaluation

During strategic planning, mega-level results should be analyzed before or while establishing macro-level needs, which should be analyzed before investigating micro-level needs and selecting appropriate means. However, not all corporate businesses will consider mega-level needs as an initial point for conducting their needs assessments. In that case, the mega-level outcomes can be used for an ethical check. For example, changing chemicals in a new pesticide might help increase the organizational bottomline, but the pesticide might be harmful to a certain species. Therefore, the company might decide not to use the chemicals in the new pesticide product for ethical reasons.

When compared to the OEM structure, Kirkpatrick's evaluation model does not include the mega-level outcomes (Kaufman, 1997; Kaufman & Keller, 1994). Table 22 presents a comparison between Kaufman's OEM structure and Kirkpatrick's four-level model of evaluation and the flow of strategic planning and evaluation (based on the information in Table 12). Figure 31 illustrates how the OEM structure fits into the steps of the HPT model.

Table 22. A Comparison between Kaufman's OEM and Kirkpatrick's Evaluation Model and the Flow of Strategic Planning and Evaluation

Goals and Objectives (Kaufman's OEM)	Kirkpatrick's Four-Level Model of Evaluation
Societal goals (Mega-level needs) ↓	Societal impact (not included) ↑
1. Organizational goals (Macro-level needs) ↓	8. Results ↑
2. Performance objectives (Micro-level needs) ↓	7. Behavior ↑
3. Instructional objectives (Micro-level needs) ↓	6. Learning ↑
4. Motivational objectives (Means: Inputs and processes)	5. Reaction ↑

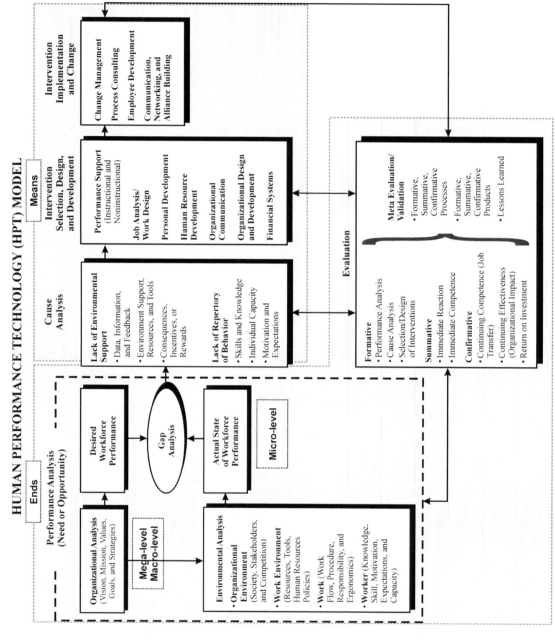

Figure 31. Means and ends (mega, macro and micro levels) in the HPT model: Adapted from human performance technology (HPT) model.

References

Banathy, B. H. (1968). *Instructional systems*. Palo Alto, CA: Fearon Publishers.

Banathy, B. H. (1992). *A systems view of education: Concepts and principles for effective practice*. Englewood Cliffs, NJ: Educational Technology Publications.

Kaufman, R. (1972). *Educational system planning*. Englewood Cliffs, NJ: Prentice-Hall.

Kaufman, R. (1983). A holistic planning model: A system approach for improving organizational effectiveness and impact. *Performance and Instruction, 22*(8), 3–12.

Kaufman, R. (1988, September). Preparing useful performance indicators. *Training & Development, 42*, 80–83.

Kaufman, R. (1992a, May). 6 steps to strategic success. *Training & Development, 46*, 107–112.

Kaufman, R. (1992b). *Strategic planning plus: An organizational guide* (rev. ed.). Newbury Park, CA: Sage.

Kaufman, R. (1994). A needs assessment audit. *Performance and Instruction, 33*(2), 14–16.

Kaufman, R. (1997). Avoiding the "dumbing down" of human performance improvement. *Performance Improvement, 36*(5), 22–24.

Kaufman, R. (2000). *Mega planning: Practical tools for organizational success*. Thousand Oaks, CA: Sage.

Kaufman, R., Johnston, J. C., & Nickols, F. K. (1979, September). Organizational planning and conventional wisdom. *Training & Development, 33*, 70–76.

Kaufman, R., & Keller, J. (1994). Levels of evaluation: Beyond Kirkpatrick. *Human Resource Development Quarterly, 5*(4), 371–380.

Kaufman, R., Oakley-Browne, H., Watkins, R., & Leigh, D. (2003). *Strategic planning for success: Aligning people, performance, and payoffs*. San Francisco: Jossey-Bass/Pfeiffer.

Kaufman, R., & Stakenas, R. G. (1981). Needs assessment and holistic planning. *Educational Leadership, 38*(8), 612–616.

Kaufman, R., & Thiagarajan, S. (1987). Identifying and specifying requirements for instruction. In R. M. Gagné (Ed.), *Instructional technology: Foundations* (pp. 113–140). Hillsdale, NJ: Lawrence Erlbaum Associates.

Merriam-Webster's collegiate dictionary (11th ed.). (2003). Springfield, MA: Merriam-Webster.

Watkins, R., & Kaufman, R. (1996). An update on relating needs assessment and needs analysis. *Performance Improvement, 35*(10), 10–13.

Organizational Behavior

Understanding Organizational Behavior

Psychology	**psy·chol·o·gy** \sī-ˈkä-lə-ˌjē\ *n, pl* –**gies** 1: the science of mind and behavior 2: a: the mental or behavioral characteristics of an individual or group b: the study of mind and behavior in relation to a particular field of knowledge or activity 3: a theory or system of psychology (Merriam-Webster's Collegiate Dictionary, 2003, p. 1004)
Industrial and organizational psychology	Educational psychology is the study of human learning in educational settings. It has provided foundational principles of human learning to the practice of instructional technology. The field of industrial and organizational (I/O) psychology shares some of its principles and concepts with the field of educational psychology, but the focus is different. I/O psychology is concerned with the study of work behavior in the context of business and industry. The need to improve efficiency in productivity was a major force in the development of the discipline during the early era of I/O psychology. Muchinsky (2000) explains: The merging of psychology with applied interests and concern for increasing industrial efficiency was the ingredient for the emergence of I/O psychology. By 1910 "industrial psychology" (the "organizational" appendage did not become official until 1970) was a legitimate specialty area of psychology. (p. 9)
Social psychology	Social psychology is based on concepts derived from psychology and sociology, focusing on the influence of people on each other in social environments and investigating the phenomenon of *change*—that is, how to initiate and manage change through barriers (Robbins, 2000). Research in social psychology is concerned with work-related behaviors and attitudes, group dynamics, and leadership (Greenberg & Baron, 1997).
Applications of the works of Taylor, Lewin, and Herzberg to HPT practice	This chapter provides an overview of several theories derived from the fields of industrial and organizational psychology and social psychology, such as Frederick Taylor's scientific management theory; the Hawthorne studies conducted by many researchers including Elton Mayo; Kurt Lewin's field theory; and Frederick Herzberg's motivation-hygiene theory. These prominent figures worked prior to the existence of the field of human performance technology and were not human performance technologists, but their theories and research findings have had a substantial impact on and hold implications for current HPT practice in regard to understanding human behavior and improving performance in work environments.

Frederick Taylor's Scientific Management

The father
of scientific
management

Frederick Winslow Taylor (1856–1915), known as *the father of scientific management*, started his career as an apprentice at the Midvale Steel Company in Philadelphia in the late 19th century. (He later became a foreman, chief engineer, and manager.) He earned a mechanical engineering degree from the Stevens Institute of Technology in New Jersey by completing correspondence courses while he was working at Midvale. He developed an interest in improving work efficiency during his early days at Midvale (Wrege & Greenwood, 1991).

After leaving the Midvale Steel Company, Taylor worked as a consultant to several other companies, including the Bethlehem Steel Corporation. In his book *The Principles of Scientific Management* (1911/1998), Taylor describes his pig-iron experiments conducted at Bethlehem Steel, where he engineered human performance and improved efficiency through scientifically designed management techniques.

Principles of
scientific
management

While working at the Midvale Steel Company, Taylor (1911/1998) identified problems with the previous "initiative and incentive" management style, especially with the "soldiering behavior" among workers. He proposed a scientific management method as a solution to the problem:

- Performance problem: "The great loss which the whole country is suffering through inefficiency in almost all of our daily acts" (p. iv).

- Cause: "The defective systems of management which are in common use, and which make it necessary for each workman to soldier, or work slowly, in order that he may protect his own best interests" (p. 4).

- Solution: "The remedy for this inefficiency lies in systematic management" (p. iv).

Taylor (1911/1998) argued that "the principal object of management should be to secure the maximum prosperity for the employer, coupled with the maximum prosperity for each employee" (p. 1) and "the best management is a true science, resting upon clearly defined laws, rules, and principles, as a foundation" (p. vi). He explained that managers who adopt the systematic management method would adhere to the following four principles, which are now known as *the foundational principles of scientific management*:

First. They develop a science for each element of a man's work, which replaces the old rule-of-thumb method.

Second. They scientifically select and then train, teach, and develop the workman, whereas in the past he chose his own work and trained himself as best he could.

Third. They heartily cooperate with the men so as to insure all of the work being done in accordance with the principles of the science which has been developed.

Fourth. There is an almost equal division of the work and the responsibility between the management and the workmen. The management take[s] over all work for which they are better fitted than the workmen, while in the past almost all of the work and the greater part of the responsibility were thrown upon the men. (p. 15)

From scientific management to behavior engineering	Frederick Taylor's work precedes the work of Thomas Gilbert by about 70 years, but many similarities are found in the two men's theories. This may be because Gilbert was influenced by Frederick Taylor (Dean, 1997). The similarities can be illustrated by summarizing Taylor's work at the Bethlehem Steel Company using Gilbert's first three leisurely theorems (Chyung, 2005a). • Taylor emphasized the importance of producing improved performance at reduced costs, which is similar to Gilbert's first leisurely theorem about producing *worthy performance*. In fact, Taylor was hired as a consultant to the Bethlehem Steel Corporation because the company had difficulty lowering production costs to meet the federal government's request for lower prices for products (Wrege & Greenwood, 1991). • Taylor also measured and used the best possible level of performance as the standard and tried to improve the average performance to the best performance level. For example, the pig-iron handlers at Bethlehem were loading an average of 12½ tons per worker each day, but Taylor found out from his analysis that the first-class pig-iron handler could handle about 48 tons per day. The gap between the two was significant. This is similar to how Gilbert compared the *typical* performance to the *exemplary* performance to measure the performance gap in his second leisurely theorem. • All six factors that Gilbert presented in his third leisurely theorem (a.k.a., the behavior engineering model) are found in Taylor's work.

However, unlike the specific sequence Gilbert proposed, it appears that Taylor's methods were utilized in a different order, as shown in Figure 32.

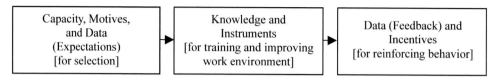

Figure 32. The sequence of Taylor's methods.

More specifically:

1. **Capacity.** High-performing pig-iron handlers were selected as potential "high-priced men" based on their physical conditions and psychological conditions, such as their ambition, diligence, and habits.
2. **Motives.** It was assumed that the workers' motives for agreeing to follow the scientific management practice were to earn monetary incentives and self-respect by becoming high-priced (or first-class) men.
3. **Data (expectations).** The desired performance and its consequence were clearly explained to workers. The selected workers were told that if they followed the directions, they would be able to become high-value workers who could earn $1.85 a day, instead of the usual $1.15 a day.
4. **Knowledge.** Workers were provided with step-by-step training, in some cases along with written directions that were based on a carefully conducted task analysis.
5. **Instruments.** Instead of selecting and using their own shovels, shovelers were provided with 8 to 10 newly designed and improved shovels for handling specific types of material.
6. **Data (feedback).** Immediate feedback was provided to workers to manage high-level performance. For illiterate workers, colored papers were used for different feedback. Receiving a white paper would mean that the worker met the standard and earned the promised wage, but a yellow paper would mean that the worker did not meet the standard and failed to earn the high wage.
7. **Incentives.** As promised, high-priced men received a 62 percent increase in income (from $1.15 to $1.85) for improving their performance (from handling 12½ tons to handling 48 tons). In addition to the monetary incentive, they were provided with other types of incentives, such as possible promotions, shorter working hours, and better work conditions.

The Hawthorne Studies

Factoring in human motives

Frederick Taylor and his followers advocated the importance of applying scientific principles to industrial management. Taylor in his scientific management theory emphasized the systematic organization of work tasks, as well as the selection of workers based on their physical capabilities and psychological attributes. Taylor stressed the need for factoring in human motives that influence workers and the use of non-monetary incentives (such as appealing to their pride and self-respect), as well as monetary incentives (such as increased pay).

Taylor's work was one of the pioneering events during the late 19th century and the early 20th century that provided industry leaders with an understanding about the need to apply social and behavioral sciences to the solutions of problems in the industry (Gillespie, 1991).

The Hawthorne studies

The Hawthorne studies were also instrumental in disseminating a new philosophy and practice of industrial management that is grounded in objective scientific research (Gillespie, 1991). It was between 1924 and 1932 when the Western Electric Company's Hawthorne Works in Chicago conducted a series of experiments. The original purpose of the studies was to measure effects of variables in the work environment on productivity. But instead, the studies helped reveal complex aspects of workers' individual and group behaviors that influence their performance (Roethlisberger & Dickson, 1939).

The first series of experiments, the so-called *illumination experiments*, were conducted in collaboration with the National Research Council of the National Academy of Sciences (Cass & Zimmer, 1975). The purpose of the experiments was to measure the effect of changes in illumination on worker productivity. The intensity of illumination was increased or decreased to see how the changes affected productivity. However, the researchers were puzzled to find out that the results were inconclusive: the productivity of the test group increased and decreased in no relation to the changes in light, and the control group working without any experimental changes also increased productivity as much as the test group did. They concluded that light was only a minor factor among many other factors that affected performance, and believed that they failed to control other factors to measure the effect of the light factor (Roethlisberger & Dickson, 1939). More importantly, the researchers realized that the hidden variable that influenced the changes in performance was human motive: workers improved productivity because they thought they were expected to do so, or they decreased productivity because they felt suspicious of the investigators' intentions. After the illumination experiments, the National Research Council withdrew from the studies, and a group of researchers led by Harvard professor Elton Mayo was invited to take over the remaining studies (Cass & Zimmer, 1975).

The second series of studies was conducted with a small number of female operators in the relay assembly test room who were separated from the regular working force. Conditions such as changes in wage incentives, schedules of rest periods, and lengths of working hours were imposed on the small group, and an observer was stationed in the room to record the performance outputs. After several years of experimentation, the researchers concluded that there was no clear correlation between working conditions and performance outcomes. The operators steadily increased their performance outputs, regardless of the numerous changes introduced to the work conditions. One widely accepted interpretation of the results is that the operators knew they were a special study group (a novelty effect) and responded to the tests with increased productivity (also known as *the Hawthorne effect*). Based on the experiments, the researchers came to realize that changes in working conditions did not directly lead to results. Rather, they influenced changes in mental attitudes in the group, which in turn influenced results (Mayo, 1960).

Another experiment was conducted with male workers in the bank wiring observation room. Unlike what was observed with the female workers in the relay assembly test room, male workers in the bank wiring observation room restricted their performance outputs or incorrectly reported their output to the group chief in order to meet collective output norms. Individual workers were influenced by group pressure via sarcasm, name-calling (e.g., "rate-buster," "chiseler," or "squealer"), and "binging" (i.e., hitting a person on the upper arm with a fist) (Roethlisberger & Dickson, 1939). A similar example of a group norm affecting performance in a negative way is the *systemic soldiering* behavior described in Taylor's book *The Principles of Scientific Management* (1911/1998).

Implications of the Hawthorne studies for HPT practice	The Hawthorne studies offer several practical implications to performance improvement professionals:

1. Selected interventions do not always produce expected results. There can be hidden variables that influence the results. Practitioners should keep in mind this information while conducting research and evaluations.
2. Not all incentives need to be tangible and monetary. Non-monetary incentives such as paying special attention to performers can improve their performance levels. Performance improvement practitioners can use this information while selecting or designing appropriate interventions.
3. Group standards influence the behavior of individual workers, sometimes more so than monetary rewards do (Robbins, 2000). The norm developed by a group can influence the behavior of individual group members negatively as well as positively. This information can be helpful to practitioners who are investigating factors that influence group dynamics during a cause analysis phase or a change management phase. |

Kurt Lewin's Field Theory

Group dynamics based on Gestalt psychology	Kurt Lewin (1890–1947), born and educated in Germany, was a professor of psychology at the University of Berlin until 1932. Then he moved to the United States and served as a faculty member at Stanford University and Cornell University. Lewin was also the director of the Research Center for Group Dynamics at Massachusetts Institute of Technology (Lewin, 1935, 1936). Lewin's work on group dynamics is considered one of the most important contributions to social psychology. He conducted research on human behavior with a focus on "dynamic interactions" among members of the group, rather than studying individual human behavior alone. Lewin's theory of group dynamics was based on Gestalt psychology, which emerged in Germany during the early decades of the 20th century. The term *Gestalt* means "a system whose parts are dynamically connected in such a way that a change of one part results in a change of all other parts" (Lewin, 1936, p. 218).
Field theory	Although Lewin studied Gestalt psychology, he soon extended his focus on perceptual phenomena and investigated the interactions between environmental stimuli and a person's individual characteristics, and the resulting behavioral outcomes. He explained that the fundamental psychological importance is placed on "the direct relationship between the momentary state of the individual and the structure of his psychological environment" (p. 76). He expressed this concept with the following formula: $B = f (P\ E)$, which likely influenced Thomas Gilbert in formulating his third leisurely theorem (Dean, 1997). Lewin wrote in 1935:

> To understand or predict the psychological behavior (B) one has to determine for every kind of psychological event (actions, emotions, expressions, etc.) the momentary whole situation, that is, the momentary structure and the state of the person (P) and of the psychological environment (E). $B = f (P\ E)$. (p. 79)

In his theory, usually referred to as *field theory*, Lewin (1935) explains that a *field of force* refers to the type of force that exists in an individual at the moment the individual is involved in social interactions. Two types of forces exist—*driving* forces and *restraining* forces. Lewin (1948) explains the two types of forces in regard to a group situation:

> The sources of the forces toward the group may be manifold: perhaps the individual feels attracted to other members of the group, perhaps the other members draw him in, maybe he is interested in the goal of the group or feels in accord with its ideology, or he may prefer this group to being alone. Similarly, the

forces away from the group may be the result of any sort of dis-
agreeable features of the group itself, or they may be an expression of
the greater attractiveness of an outside group. (pp. 190–191)

Lewin (1935) explains that fields of forces create *changes* in physical
systems and that the dynamic aspects of the changes in turn create a phenom-
enon called *equilibrium*:

> 1. The process moves in the direction of a state of equilibrium only
> for the *system as a whole*. . . . 2. A state of equilibrium in a system
> does not mean, further, that the system is without tension. Systems
> can, on the contrary, also come to equilibrium in a state of tension
> (e.g., a spring under tension or a container with gas under
> pressure). (p. 58)

In other words, his field theory explains that organizations and individual
performers constantly encounter dynamic changes due to the fields of forces
and equilibrium that they experience.

Application of field theory to HPT practice: force-field analysis

Lewin's field theory has been transformed into an analysis tool, usually
labeled *force-field analysis*. This method can be used during the change
management phase or when starting the intervention selection phase in the
HPT model, since implementation of new interventions would likely result in
some types of changes in the organization, causing driving forces and
restraining forces to be created. The force-field analysis would help reveal
the nature of the forces and determine change management strategies.

For example, recall the hypothetical situation described in Chapter 9, where
an engineering consulting company decided to launch a company-wide
e-learning initiative. This initiative would instigate a substantial change in
the organization. Through methods such as focus groups, surveys, and interviews, the organization will be able to uncover specific driving forces and
restraining forces regarding the change, as illustrated in Table 23, which will
help when developing effective change management strategies.

Table 23. A Simple Example of a Force-Field Analysis

Driving Forces	Change: A Company-Wide E-learning Initiative	Restraining Forces
• Engineers want to excel • Timely learning and performance • Cost-effective learning solutions	⟶ ⟵	• Costs for the LMS • Engineers are not familiar with e-learning • Resistance to technology-driven learning solutions

Frederick Herzberg's Motivation-Hygiene Theory

Motivation
factors vs.
hygiene factors

Before Frederick Herzberg (1923–2000) developed his motivation-hygiene theory, the traditional view of job satisfaction and dissatisfaction was that the opposite of job satisfaction was job dissatisfaction, and the opposite of job dissatisfaction was job satisfaction. In other words, it was assumed that removing the factors that dissatisfy workers would satisfy them and removing the factors that satisfy workers would dissatisfy them.

Herzberg proposed that this was not true. His theory was that the opposite of satisfaction is not dissatisfaction, but *no satisfaction*, and the opposite of dissatisfaction is not satisfaction, but *no dissatisfaction*. He and his colleagues researched this idea and revealed two separate sets of factors that cause job satisfaction and job dissatisfaction: motivation factors and hygiene factors (Herzberg, 1966, 1968, 1987; Herzberg, Mausner, & Snyderman, 1959).

He chose the term *hygiene factors* to be "analogous to the medical use of the term hygiene, in which health hazards are removed from the environment to prevent diseases rather than to cure them" (Whitsett & Winslow, 1967, p. 393). The term *motivation factors* refers to growth and improvement after the hazardous ingredients have been removed. The components of the two factors are listed in Table 24.

Table 24. Hygiene and Motivation Factors (Herzberg, 1968, 1987)

Hygiene Factors	Motivation Factors
• Working conditions • Policies and administrative practices • Supervision • Interpersonal relations • Salary (all forms of financial compensation) • Status • Job security • Personal life	• Achievement • Recognition • Responsibility • Work itself • Growth • Advancement Based on this model, Herzberg and his colleagues believed that "job enrichment" is a managerial solution to motivate workers.

Application
of two-factor
theory to HPT
practice

Herzberg's theory and research in understanding job satisfaction and dissatisfaction is similar to the principle behind Thorndike's law of effect with satisfiers and annoyers (see Chapter 2). Herzberg's motivation-hygiene theory can be used during a cause analysis as a framework for investigating factors that influence job satisfaction and dissatisfaction.

For example, HPT practitioners may apply Herzberg's two-factor theory while using Gilbert's behavior engineering model to diagnose behavioral deficiencies. The two categories of Herzberg's theory are often explained with a dichotomy of job-content (intrinsic) and job-context (environmental)—that is, motivation factors tend to be related to job content that promotes intrinsic motivation, and hygiene factors tend to address the environmental context on the job.

When comparing this dichotomy of Herzberg's theory to Gilbert's behavior engineering model, the conditions of hygiene factors seem to parallel the category of environmental supports (i.e., incentives), and the conditions of motivation factors seem to parallel the category of a person's repertory of behavior (i.e., motives). Therefore, a survey instrument can be developed based on Herzberg's two-factor theory to investigate the effects of incentives and motives on human performance (the third column of Gilbert's behavior engineering model, as shown in Table 25).

Table 25. Behavior Engineering Model

	Information	**Instrumentation**	**Motivation**
Environmental Supports	1. Data	2. Instruments	3. Incentives
Person's Repertory of Behavior	4. Knowledge	5. Capacity	6. Motives

Note. From *Human competence: Engineering worthy performance* (p. 88) by T. Gilbert. Copyright © 1996, 2006 by the International Society for Performance Improvement. Reprinted with permission of John Wiley & Sons, Inc.

Herzberg's two-factor theory can also be applied as a theoretical framework for analyzing factors in learning environments that affect learners' feelings of satisfaction and dissatisfaction.

For example, Chyung and Vachon (2005) studied profiles of satisfying and dissatisfying factors in an instructor-led e-learning environment, using the two-factor theory as a theoretical framework.

They found out that the major motivation factors included the following:
1. The learning content itself
2. The instructor's teaching methods or styles
3. The instructor's subject matter expertise
4. The types of learning activities

The major hygiene factors that they found included the following:
1. Instructional directions and expectations
2. The instructor's level of participation in discussions

The researchers recommended that to be systematically proactive, e-learning institutions should try to remove dissatisfying factors before or while adding satisfying factors for two reasons: the presence of hygiene factors would still cause learner dissatisfaction, despite the effects of motivational factors; and continued abundance of hygiene factors may cause undesirable consequences, such as abandonment or dropouts (also see Chyung, 2005b).

As shown in Figure 33, the findings of Chyung and Vachon's research can be utilized within the OEM framework (Kaufman, 2000) in order to influence learners' satisfaction toward the e-learning environment, as well as learning outcomes (i.e., products). This will in turn affect the course-level or program-level retention rates (i.e., outputs) and will eventually help continuous development of e-learning in higher education.

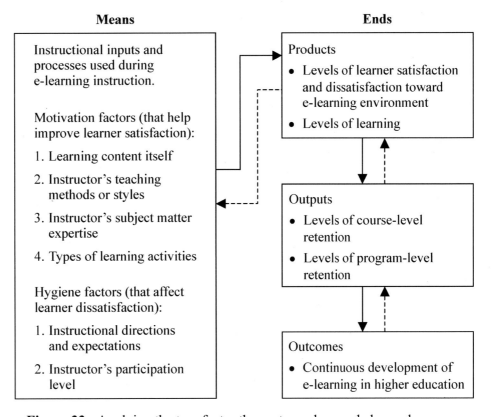

Figure 33. Applying the two-factor theory to analyze and change learner satisfaction and dissatisfaction, and to produce desirable results.

Theory to Practice

Applications of theories and research findings to HPT practice

Taylor's scientific management, the Hawthorne studies, Lewin's field theory, Herzberg's two-factor theory, and Likert's development of the Likert scale are good examples of theories and research findings derived from industrial and organizational psychology and social psychology that provide HPT professionals with foundational frameworks for their practice. As shown in Figure 34, Herzberg's two-factor theory can be used during a cause analysis to reveal various factors that affect job satisfaction and job dissatisfaction. Force-field analysis can be used during a change management phase in order to measure driving and restraining forces toward the selected intervention (i.e., a change) and to develop strategies to facilitate the implementation process. Force-field analysis can also be used as part of a cause analysis tool in conjunction with Gilbert's behavior engineering model to weigh the relative degrees of individual factors that cause a performance gap (see Chevalier, 2003).

The two categories in force-field analysis are similar to the dichotomous structure used in a SWOT analysis that measures strengths, weaknesses, opportunities, and threats in pursuit of a strategic goal. The development of the SWOT analysis is credited to Albert Humphrey, who led a project at Stanford Research Institute (Worldwide TAM, n.d.). Strengths and opportunities fall into the category of driving forces that are internal and external to the organization, whereas weaknesses and threats would be restraining forces that are internal and external to the organization (see Table 26). Both force-field analysis and SWOT analysis intend to generate strategies to facilitate driving forces and to overcome restraining forces toward the change.

Table 26. SWOT Analysis and Force-Field Analysis

	Internal to Organization	**External to Organization**
Driving Forces	Strengths	Opportunities
Restraining Forces	Weaknesses	Threats

In addition to the information introduced in this book, there are many other theories and research findings derived from industrial and organizational psychology and social psychology that can be used during the performance improvement processes. Therefore, HPT practitioners are encouraged to engage in the study of theories and research in industrial and organizational psychology or social psychology so that they can equip themselves with a variety of tools for improving human performance.

HUMAN PERFORMANCE TECHNOLOGY (HPT) MODEL

Performance Analysis (Need or Opportunity)

Organizational Analysis (Vision, Mission, Values, Goals, and Strategies)

Environmental Analysis
- **Organizational Environment** (Society, Stakeholders, and Competition)
- **Work Environment** (Resources, Tools, Human Resources Policies)
- **Work** (Work Flow, Procedure, Responsibility, and Ergonomics)
- **Worker** (Knowledge, Skill, Motivation, Expectations, and Capacity)

Desired Workforce Performance

Gap Analysis

Actual State of Workforce Performance

Cause Analysis

Lack of Environmental Support
- Data, Information, and Feedback
- Environment Support, Resources, and Tools
- Consequences, Incentives, or Rewards

Lack of Repertory of Behavior
- Skills and Knowledge
- Individual Capacity
- Motivation and Expectations

Intervention Selection, Design, and Development

Performance Support (Instructional and Noninstructional)

Job Analysis/ Work Design

Personal Development

Human Resource Development

Organizational Communication

Organizational Design and Development

Financial Systems

Intervention Implementation and Change

Change Management

Process Consulting

Employee Development

Communication, Networking, and Alliance Building

Force-Field Analysis

Two-Factor Theory

Evaluation

Formative
- Performance Analysis
- Cause Analysis
- Selection/Design of Interventions

Summative
- Immediate Reaction
- Immediate Competence

Confirmative
- Continuing Competence (Job Transfer)
- Continuing Effectiveness (Organizational Impact)
- Return on Investment

Meta Evaluation/ Validation
- Formative, Summative, Confirmative Processes
- Formative, Summative, Confirmative Products
- Lessons Learned

Figure 34. Utilizing theories and research findings during the steps of the HPT model: Adapted from human performance technology (HPT) model.

References

Cass, E. L., & Zimmer, F. G. (Eds.) (1975). *Man and work in society: A report on the symposium held on the occasion of the 50th anniversary of the original Hawthorne Studies.* New York: Van Nostrand Reinhold Company.

Chevalier, R. (2003). Updating the behavior engineering model. *Performance Improvement Journal, 42*(5), 8–14.

Chyung, S. Y. (2005a). Human performance technology: From Taylor's scientific management to Gilbert's behavior engineering model. *Performance Improvement Journal, 44*(1), 23–28.

Chyung, S. Y. (2005b). Understanding different categories of attrition in distance education programs. In Rogers, P. (Ed.), *The encyclopedia of distance learning* (Vol. 4, pp. 1917–1925). Hershey, PA: IDEA Group.

Chyung, S. Y., & Vachon, M. (2005). An investigation of the profiles of satisfying and dissatisfying factors in e-learning. *Performance Improvement Quarterly, 18*(2), 97–113.

Dean, P. J. (1997). Thomas F. Gilbert, Ph.D. Engineering Performance with or without training. In P. J. Dean, & D. E. Ripley (Eds.), *Performance improvement pathfinders: Models for organizational learning systems* (Vol. 1, pp. 45–64). Silver Spring, MD: The International Society for Performance Improvement.

Gilbert, T. F. (1996). *Human competence: Engineering worthy performance* (Tribute ed.). Washington, D.C.: The International Society for Performance Improvement.

Gillespie, R. (1991). *Manufacturing knowledge: A history of the Hawthorne experiments.* Cambridge: Cambridge University Press.

Greenberg, J., & Baron, R. A. (1997). *Behavior in organization* (6th ed.). Upper Saddle River, NJ: Prentice-Hall.

Herzberg, F. (1966). *The work and the nature of man.* Cleveland, OH: The World Publishing Company.

Herzberg, F. (1968). One more time: How do you motivate employees? *Harvard Business Review, 46*(1), 53–63.

Herzberg, F. (1987). HRD classic: One more time: How do you motivate employees? *Harvard Business Review, 65*(5), 109–120.

Herzberg, F., Mausner, B., & Snyderman, B. (1959). *The motivation to work.* New York: John Wiley & Sons, Inc.

Kaufman, R. (2000). *Mega planning: Practical tools for organizational success.* Thousand Oaks, CA: Sage.

Lewin, K. (1935). *A dynamic theory of personality: Selected papers* (D. K. Adams & K. E. Zener, Trans.). New York: McGraw-Hill Book Company.

Lewin, K. (1936). *Principle of topological psychology* (F. Heider & G. M. Heider, Trans.). New York: McGraw-Hill Book Company.

Lewin, K. (1948). *Resolving social conflicts* (Edited by G. W. Lewin). New York: Harper & Brothers.

Mayo, E. (1960). *The human problems of an industrial civilization.* New York: The Viking Press.

Merriam-Webster's collegiate dictionary (11th ed.). (2003). Springfield, MA: Merriam-Webster.

Muchinsky, P. M. (2000). *Psychology applied to work: An introduction to industrial and organizational psychology* (6th ed.). Belmont, CA: Wadsworth.

Roethlisberger, F. J., & Dickson, W. J. (1939). *Management and the workers: An account of a research program conducted by the Western Electric Company, Hawthorne Works, Chicago.* Cambridge: Harvard University Press.

Robbins, S. P. (1998). *Organizational behavior* (8th ed.). Upper Saddle River, NJ: Prentice Hall.

Robbins, S. P. (2000). *Essentials of organizational behavior* (6th ed.). Upper Saddle River, NJ: Prentice Hall.

Taylor, F. (1998). *The principles of scientific management.* Mineola, New York: Dover Publications. (Original work published 1911)

Whitsett, D. A., & Winslow, E. K. (1967). An analysis of studies critical of the motivator-hygiene theory. *Personnel Psychology, 10*(4), 391–415.

Worldwide TAM (n.d.). *Albert S Humphrey.* Retrieved June 1, 2007, from http://www.worldwidetam.com/Humphsprofile.htm

Wrege, C. D., & Greenwood, R. G. (1991). *Frederick W. Taylor the father of scientific management: Myth and reality.* Homewood, IL: Business One Irwin.

Chapter

Summing Up

The Relationship between IT and HPT

Instructional technology and human performance technology

Instructional technology is the systematic and systemic application of theories, concepts, principles, and methods to learning situations in order to produce improvement in human learning.

The means used in instructional technology is instruction, and the end result is the desired level of improvement in human learning. To produce the expected end result, the means (instruction) should be systematically and systemically analyzed, designed, developed, implemented, and evaluated. This is referred to as a *technology of instruction.*

Human performance technology is the systematic and systemic application of theories, concepts, principles, and methods to work situations in order to produce improvement in human learning and behavior, organizational success, and/or organizational impact on its society.

The means used in human performance technology include instruction and noninstructional interventions such as incentives, selection of workers, and work-flow redesign. The end results are the desired levels of improvement in human learning and behavior, organizational success, and/or organizational impact on its society. To produce the expected end results, the means should be selected by a careful in-depth analysis and designed, developed, implemented, and evaluated in systematic and systemic manners. This is a *technology of performance improvement.*

Instructional and performance technologists

Instructional technologists and human performance technologists are professionals who employ the *technologies of instruction and performance improvement* to help achieve desired end results. To be qualified as instructional and performance technologists, they are expected to possess a competent level of knowledge, skills, and attitudes that enable them to select and utilize various *technologies* of instruction and performance improvement and to achieve desired end results. Acquiring such competence starts with learning about the historical and theoretical foundations of the fields and understanding the fundamental principles that are applied to practice.

Historical and theoretical foundations of the fields

This chapter provides a summary of historical and theoretical relationships between the field of instructional technology and the field of human performance technology. It also introduces a couple of organizations in the fields of instructional technology and human performance technology, such as the American Society for Training and Development (ASTD) and the International Society for Performance Improvement (ISPI), and provides suggestions to practitioners for building foundational knowledge.

The Historical and Theoretical Relationships

The parent-child relationship

The relationship between the field of instructional technology and the field of human performance technology can be explained in several ways.

First, historically the field of instructional technology is a parent to the field of human performance technology. Instructional technology as a profession started to be recognized during and after World War II. The field of instructional technology consumes foundational principles of human learning and behavior developed by educational psychologists. Figure 35 illustrates the influence of educational psychology on the development of the field of instructional technology and shows the names of several main contributors.

1910   '20s   '30s   '40s   '50s   '60s   '70s   '80s   '90s   2000   →

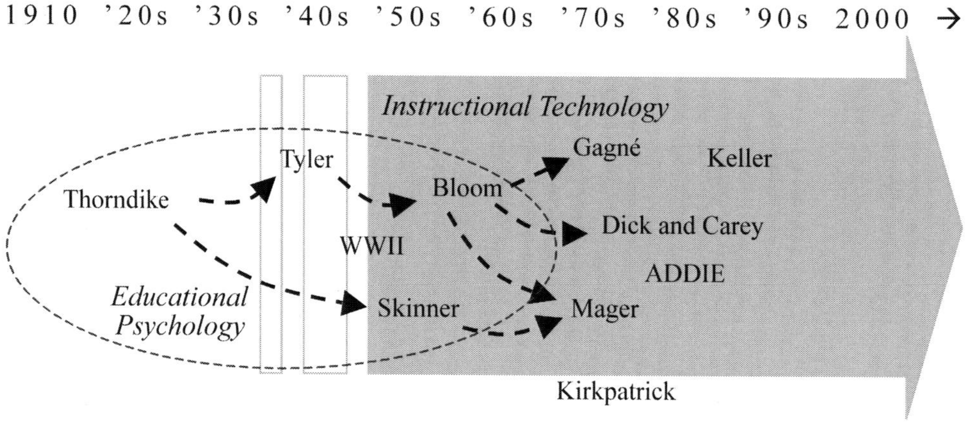

Figure 35. The development of instructional technology as a profession.

Note: The contributors' names are listed on the approximate locations of the timeline, and the arrows indicate an example of their influence.

Human performance technology as a profession grew out of the instructional technology field during the 1960s and 1970s, based on the conceptual realization among leading practitioners that instruction alone would not be a sufficient solution to *all* types of performance problems. Several main practitioners in the field of instructional technology, such as Robert Mager and Thomas Gilbert, also contributed to the development of the HPT field. Industrial and organizational psychology and social psychology are not the parents to the HPT field, but they provided the foundational ground work that supports the theory and practice of human performance technology. Thomas Gilbert, known as the father of performance technology, was influenced by pioneering scientists in other fields, such as Frederick Taylor, Kurt Lewin, and B. F. Skinner. The HPT field became better known to the public during the 1980s and 1990s. Figure 36 illustrates the development of the field of human performance technology and lists the names of several main contributors.

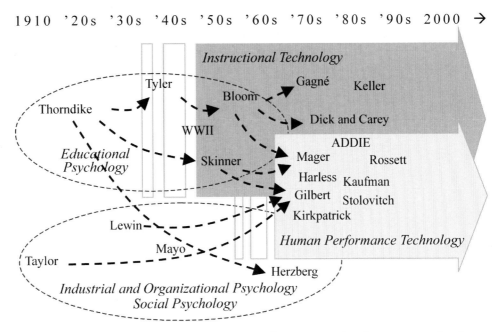

Figure 36. The development of human performance technology as a profession.

Note: The contributors' names are listed on the approximate locations of the timeline, and the arrows point to an example of their influence.

The big brother and little brother (or big sister and little sister) relationship

Second, the field of instructional technology and the field of human performance technology are different in scope. Simply put, instructional technology focuses on improving learning outcomes, and human performance technology focuses on improving performance or organizational outcomes, as well as learning outcomes. Therefore, the practice of human performance technology (such as needs assessment) starts before the practice of instructional technology. In addition, human performance technology utilizes a larger number of interventions, including instruction. In this sense, the field of human performance technology can be thought of as a big brother or sister to the field of instructional technology, as illustrated in Figure 37.

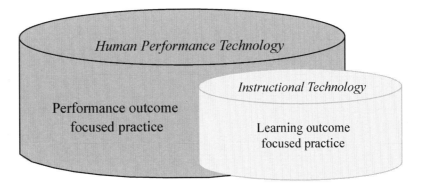

Figure 37. A sibling-like relationship between IT and HPT.

To continue our "sibling" analogy, it can be said that the practice of instructional technology and the practice of human performance technology share the same "DNA structure," represented by ADDIE. Several examples are shown in Table 27.

Table 27. The "ADDIE" DNA Structure Found in IT and HPT Practices.

	Instructional Technology	**Human Performance Technology**
Analysis	Conduct a goal analysis, a task analysis, a learner analysis, etc.	Conduct a needs assessment, a cause analysis, etc.
Design	Design instructional objectives and lessons	Design performance objectives
Development	Develop instructional materials	Develop performance improvement interventions
Implementation	Deliver instruction	Implement change management strategies
Evaluation	Conduct four-level evaluations	Conduct four-level evaluations

The "twin" relationship

Third, the field of instructional technology gave birth to the field of human performance technology, and human performance technology subsumes instructional technology in terms of the scope of practices. Nevertheless, the HPT field has been continuously adopting and influencing the development of the principles and practices of instructional technology, as illustrated in Figure 38. In this sense, continuous development through a reciprocal relationship between the two fields can be likened to the close connection and influence between twins.

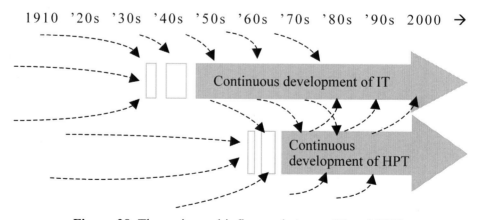

Figure 38. The reciprocal influence between IT and HPT.

Final Comments

Developing
effective
practice based
on foundational
principles

This book is intended to help practitioners in the fields of instructional technology and human performance technology build foundational knowledge of principles to help them validate and enhance their practice. The educational philosophy behind this book is illustrated in Figure 39. In addition to this book, there are other ways to build such knowledge:

- Join organizations that promote the development of communities of practice via listservs or professional conferences.
- Earn a certificate in instructional technology and/or human performance technology.
- Earn an advanced degree in instructional technology and/or human performance technology.

Professional organizations such as the American Society for Training and Development and the International Society for Performance Improvement offer workshops, conferences, and certificate programs. Colleges and universities offer graduate degrees in instructional technology and/or human performance technology. (The College of Engineering at Boise State University, for example, offers a master of science degree in instructional and performance technology and a graduate certificate in human performance technology.)

Regardless of the venues that practitioners choose in order to develop their knowledge and to advance their professional careers, it is strongly encouraged that they build solid foundations of principles and contribute to the development of the fields by engaging in evidence-based practice.

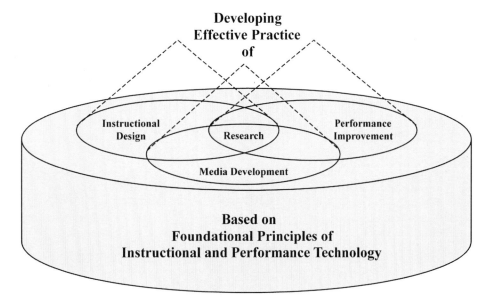

Figure 39. Developing effective practice that is based on the foundational principles of instructional and performance technology.

About the Author

Dr. Seung Youn (Yonnie) Chyung is an associate professor of the Department of Instructional and Performance Technology in the College of Engineering at Boise State University. She earned a doctor of education degree in Instructional Technology from Texas Tech University and has been teaching at Boise State University since 1996. Two of her standard graduate-level courses are Foundations of Instructional and Performance Technology and E-Learning Principles and Practices.

Dr. Chyung is the author of the book *Training Professionals' Web-Design Toolkit* (FrontPage, 2003). She has contributed chapters to several books, and over 30 papers have appeared in refereed journals or refereed conference proceedings. Research papers have been published in the *American Journal of Distance Education; Journal of Education for Business; Journal of Experimental Education; Performance Improvement Quarterly;* and *Quarterly Review of Distance Education.* She is also a frequent presenter at the annual conference of the International Society for Performance Improvement and other international conferences hosted by the Association for Educational Communications and Technology, the American Educational Research Association, and the Association for Advancement for Computing in Education. Dr. Chyung has received external grant funding from the National Science Foundations, the State of Idaho, and the International Society for Performance Improvement for implementing innovative instructional technologies and conducting research in higher education.

Dr. Chyung resides in Boise, Idaho, and can be reached at the following address: 1910 University Dr., Boise, Idaho 83725-2070, USA.